Revisualising Intersectionality

Elahe Haschemi Yekani
Magdalena Nowicka
with Tiara Roxanne

Revisualising Intersectionality

palgrave
macmillan

Elahe Haschemi Yekani
Institut für Anglistik und
Amerikanistik
Humboldt-Universität zu Berlin
Berlin, Germany

Magdalena Nowicka
Deutsches Zentrum für Integrations-
und Migrationsforschung (DeZIM)
Berlin, Germany

Tiara Roxanne
Berlin, Germany

ISBN 978-3-030-93208-4   ISBN 978-3-030-93209-1   (eBook)
https://doi.org/10.1007/978-3-030-93209-1

© The Author(s) 2022. This book is an open access publication.
Open Access This book is licensed under the terms of the Creative Commons Attribution 4.0 International License (http://creativecommons.org/licenses/by/4.0/), which permits use, sharing, adaptation, distribution and reproduction in any medium or format, as long as you give appropriate credit to the original author(s) and the source, provide a link to the Creative Commons licence and indicate if changes were made.

The images or other third party material in this book are included in the book's Creative Commons licence, unless indicated otherwise in a credit line to the material. If material is not included in the book's Creative Commons licence and your intended use is not permitted by statutory regulation or exceeds the permitted use, you will need to obtain permission directly from the copyright holder.

The use of general descriptive names, registered names, trademarks, service marks, etc. in this publication does not imply, even in the absence of a specific statement, that such names are exempt from the relevant protective laws and regulations and therefore free for general use.

The publisher, the authors and the editors are safe to assume that the advice and information in this book are believed to be true and accurate at the date of publication. Neither the publisher nor the authors or the editors give a warranty, expressed or implied, with respect to the material contained herein or for any errors or omissions that may have been made. The publisher remains neutral with regard to jurisdictional claims in published maps and institutional affiliations.

Cover Illustration: Pattern © Melisa Hasan

This Palgrave Macmillan imprint is published by the registered company Springer Nature Switzerland AG.
The registered company address is: Gewerbestrasse 11, 6330 Cham, Switzerland

Funding Acknowledgement

This book was supported by funds made available by the Volkswagen Foundation.

Acknowledgements

We are grateful for the generous financial support by the Volkswagen Foundation as well as the kind assistance by Sebastian Schneider, Tobias Schönwitz, and Pierre Schwidlinski.

We thank Ann Phoenix and all participants of the first joint workshop in preparation of this publication at the DeZIM-Institute.

We want to thank the DeZIM-Institute team, especially Nelly Holjewilken, for their support in hosting the "conversations" series. Special thanks to all of those who contributed to this format: Doireann O'Malley, Stephanie Comilang, Ashkan Sepahvand, Nine Yamamoto-Masson, Shaka McGlotten, Zander Porter and James Batchelor as well as all those who participated and discussed with us in Berlin in 2019.

We also want to extend our gratitude for the expert support by our student assistants Thao Ho and Fenja Akinde-Hummel in preparation of these events and the manuscript.

Thanks also go to our editor at Palgrave Macmillan Lina Aboujieb and editorial assistant Immy Higgins.

Elahe Haschemi Yekani wishes to thank Beatrice Michaelis, Anja Sunhyun Michaelsen, Gabriele Dietze and Noemi Yoko Molitor for their invaluable feedback and support.

Magdalena Nowicka wishes to thank Agata Lisiak for the inspiring discussions on diversity preceding the project and her family for their endless patience and support.

Tiara Roxanne wishes to thank Charlotte de Bekker, Ella Schoefer-Wulf, and Agata Lisiak for their support and presence throughout the conversations and the project as a whole.

Contents

1 **Introduction: Revisualising Intersectionality**   1
Elahe Haschemi Yekani and Magdalena Nowicka
Works Cited   8

2 **Where Difference Begins**   11
Magdalena Nowicka
Surfaces   13
A Third Race   15
The Power of Seeing   20
Intersectional Perspectives   22
Do We See What Is There?   25
How Do We See What We See?   27
Seeing Through Culture   29
Towards Intersectional Stereotyping   32
Attention: Exposure, Salience, Foregrounding   35
Conclusions   38
Works Cited   41

3 **Revisualising Intersectionality: Conversations**   55
Tiara Roxanne
Trans*   58
Sameness   62
Perception   65

	Intimacy	68
	Conclusion	73
	Works Cited	74
4	**The Ends of Visibility**	77
	Elahe Haschemi Yekani	
	Visual Culture and Intersectionality	77
	Seeing Too Little, Seeing Too Much	85
	Other Modes of Seeing, Other Modes of Being	94
	Concluding Remarks	103
	Works Cited	109
5	**Conclusion: Revising Intersectionality**	115
	Magdalena Nowicka and Elahe Haschemi Yekani	
	Works Cited	124

Index   127

List of Figures

Fig. 3.1	Doireann O'Malley, *Prototypes* film still	60
Fig. 3.2	Doireann O'Malley, *Prototypes* film still	61
Fig. 3.3	Stephanie Comilang, *Lumapit Sa Akin, Paraiso (Come to Me, Paradise)* film still	63
Fig. 3.4	Stephanie Comilang, *Lumapit Sa Akin, Paraiso (Come to Me, Paradise)* film still	64
Fig. 3.5	Ashkan Sepahvand, 27.11.2019, photo by Charlotte de Bekker	66
Fig. 3.6	Illustration by Nine Yamamoto-Masson, 27.11.2019, photo by Charlotte de Bekker	67
Fig. 3.7	James Batchelor & Zander Porter perform "Alien Intimacy", 19.12.2019, photo by Charlotte de Bekker	70
Fig. 3.8	Zander Porter, 19.12.2019, photo by Charlotte de Bekker	71
Fig. 3.9	Shaka McGlotten, Tiara Roxanne, James Batchelor, and Zander Porter, 19.12.2019, photo by Charlotte de Bekker	72

CHAPTER 1

Introduction: Revisualising Intersectionality

Elahe Haschemi Yekani and Magdalena Nowicka

Abstract The introduction to *Revisualising Intersectionality* explains the proposal for a revisualising of intersectionality as a double strategy of revising intersectionality and infusing it with a stronger focus on visual perceptions of similarity and difference to understand social stratification and inequality. Haschemi Yekani and Nowicka briefly situate the book within what by now has become the transdisciplinary field of intersectionality studies.

Keywords Intersectionality • Visuality • Visual culture • Difference

By now, numerous accounts exist of how the analysis of interlocking forms of oppression came to be associated most widely with the term "intersectionality".[1] Intersectionality has been firmly established as a transdisciplinary research paradigm in the academy and beyond. It is also often used in online and print media reports on the contemporary strand of "intersectional feminism". This increased circulation of the term as well as the academic institutionalisation of intersectionality as a research paradigm in the United States and more globally, especially in critical race theory and gender studies, has also attracted critical responses. Some scholars associate the academic success story with a depoliticisation and/or appropriation of the concept (cf. Bilge 2013; critically Nash 2019). Others caution that intersectionality runs the risk of reproducing notions of difference

© The Author(s) 2022
E. Haschemi Yekani et al., *Revisualising Intersectionality*,
https://doi.org/10.1007/978-3-030-93209-1_1

and focuses too narrowly on marginalised identities, specifically those of Black and women of colour, thus reifying, for instance, an understanding of difference *from* (white) "womanhood" rather than difference *within* groups of "women" (Puar 2012), which has been an ongoing debate in various waves and schools of feminism since at least the 1970s.

The visual metaphor of the traffic intersection as a demonstration of the effects of intersectionality was initially used by Kimberlé Williams Crenshaw (1998: 361), who is often credited with coining the term in two influential articles that deal with social justice activism and anti-discrimination legislation in the United States published in the late 1980s and early 1990s. And yet, such a metaphor tends towards the imagination of the axes of stratification as distinct and does not properly distinguish between positions and effects (Rodó-Zárate and Jorba 2020). Jennifer Nash links the term's "irresistible visuality" to its successful life inside and outside the academy. She writes,

> Given black feminists' long-standing investment in theorizing the 'interlocking' nature of power, it is worth considering how and why intersectionality came to be the preeminent term for theorizing these structures. Perhaps it is the term's irresistible visuality, its ability to be represented—even if reductively—through the crossroads metaphor that has given it a life in and beyond women's studies, and well beyond its own investment in remedying forms of juridical violence and exclusion. (Nash 2019: 11)

Many have rightfully noted that Crenshaw's manifold explanations of intersectionality should not be reduced to the visuality of the traffic intersection metaphor that contributes to the oversimplifying assumption of categories which collide. Crenshaw distinguishes intergroup and intragroup differences and speaks of intersectionality as a "provisional concept" (cf. Crenshaw 1995: 357–358, 1998: 378; Carastathis 2016: 4). Nonetheless, many intersectional research designs continue to use gender, race, and class in a simplistic manner and risk failing to address the complexity and dynamics of relationships between groups as well as the multiple differences within them which are at times tacit and hard to name. In a joint paper Sumi Cho, Leslie McCall and Kimberlé Crenshaw respond to some of these criticisms in the wake of intersectionality's many usages and highlight an understanding of intersectionality as an "analytic sensibility" (Cho et al. 2013: 795) "that is not exclusively or even primarily preoccupied with categories, identities, and subjectivities" (Cho et al. 2013: 797).

Revisualising Intersectionality explores how such an intersectional "analytic sensibility" can be expanded by considering how visuality shapes and challenges conceptions of difference, and vice versa.[2] In using the term intersectionality in the title of this book, we acknowledge the centrality of Black feminist theory and activism in spearheading conversations around the complex interactions of various modes of oppression, focusing specifically on forms of discrimination such as racism, sexism, anti-trans violence, and ableism. These are linked to the embodiment of social attributes of difference and to how regulatory discourses are inscribed onto bodies (Mirza 2013) as well as the ways in which bodies are represented. Both embodiment and representation of difference concern the perceptibility of skin pigmentation, anatomical sex and gender performativity, bodily ability but also to a lesser degree class habitus.[3] So far, the various engagements with intersectionality as a critical social theory (Collins 2019) do not address visuality explicitly, although the question of embodied differences and their social visibility remain crucial to intersectional theory building. Because the visuality of sameness and difference is always implicit in critiques of how social inequalities are embodied, it appears self-evident. But the relationship between bodily characteristics such as age or attractiveness, their social visibility, and social inequality as different dimensions of meaning is not straight-forward and cannot always be neatly captured by social categories such as race, gender, and class. Moreover, there is a discrepancy between representations of social categories, such as race and gender, and our knowledge of the non-existence of biologically discrete human races as well as the limitations of a binary conception of the sex-gender system. Instead of identifying different categories and applying them to a multi-level analysis (Winker and Degele 2011), we are especially interested in engaging with forms of visual multiplicity that do not easily fit into categories. We thus hope to avoid what Jasbir Puar describes as one of the pitfalls of intersectionality, namely the tendency to employ it as "a structural container that simply wishes the messiness of identity into a formulaic grid" (Puar 2007: 212).

Accordingly, *Revisualising Intersectionality* is concerned with a critique of the supposed visual evidentiality of categories of similarity and difference. Despite evermore creative artistic and scholarly engagements with sound, haptics, taste and smell, our emphasis on vision at the expense of other senses is motivated by the belief that visual representation holds a privileged status in relation to social recognition in an ocular-centric society. Most commonly and in everyday speech, processes of social recognition are phrased as "seeing someone" and there also exists a sometimes-naïve assumption that media representation will automatically beget greater political participation. This understanding of representation is often associated with so-called identity politics. Yet, even though visual representation and recognition are closely linked, they should not be conflated. Discrimination is frequently experienced as the non-acknowledgement of specific needs because of insufficient (political) representation. This intersectional problem cannot be alleviated simply by "positive" images and more diverse representation, as Elahe Haschemi Yekani's contribution explains in greater detail (cf. Chap. 4). Rather we are interested in the epistemological and more mundane aspects of how this affects everyday conceptions of identity and being in the world that might not always adhere to clear-cut categories but are nonetheless influenced by powerful interpellations into Otherness. Therefore, we interrogate how one might depict difference visually in a way that does justice to intersectional processes of discrimination without reifying—often binary—conceptions of difference. Visuality is understood here in the broadest possible way, not only as pertaining to (political) representation, but also to the ways in which world-making is structured visually in relation to normative imaginations and multiple interlocking inequalities but also as harbouring a potential for imagining other ways of being.

To be clear, challenging the accuracy of representation vis-à-vis reality means neither to question the existence of real differences between humans that are independent of our perception nor to question the power of representation of human bodies (Rorty 1979). It is not enough to claim that meanings—and categories—are culturally constructed. We take the materiality of different bodies and how perceptions of embodied difference affect positionalities in relation to hegemonic norms seriously. Thus, rather than simply postulate that categories are social constructs, we want to delineate how different subject positions come to matter within social hierarchies and how this is linked to visuality. Therefore, this book, on the one hand, incorporates insights from sociology, psychology, philosophy, and the interdisciplinary field of cognitive science to explain how we visually perceive physical differences and how cognition is fallible (but not accidental), processual, and dependent on who is looking in a specific spatio-temporal context (Bhaskar 1989). On the other hand, it draws on the field of visual culture studies and approaches that are associated with, but not limited to, disciplines such as gender, queer, and transgender studies as well as postcolonial and decolonial theory which often do not use the term intersectionality explicitly but have also contributed greatly to an understanding of interwoven forms of social exclusion. Moreover, adding to these various disciplinary perspectives is the belief that artistic practice and image production is an additional critical lens to intervene into habitual modes of seeing and thinking. If intersectionality research is understood as a broad analytical sensibility rather than a fixed methodology, then such an extensive transdisciplinary approach seems especially rewarding.

Consequently, we propose to expand the framework of intersectionality research to embrace a more pronounced scepticism regarding the usefulness of identity categories as analytical lenses (McCall 2005) and instead focus more on relationalities and impurity (Lugones 1994). It is our conviction that such a transdisciplinary eclectic approach can benefit the critique of power relations. In this spirit, the second term used in the title, "revisualising",[4] has an epistemological and political dimension. This neologism should be understood as a heuristic tool to help describe modes of seeing differently, as an attempt to interrupt normative visual orders based on categorisation, and thus informs our overall objective of a productive revision of intersectional analytics. Revis(ualis)ing intersectionality is not a dismissal of intersectionality, quite the opposite. It should also not be misunderstood as a naïve *un*seeing of difference. We are deeply committed to the project of intersectionality as a concern for how interwoven processes of discrimination and hierarchisation shape systems of inequality. While our call to "revis(ualis)e intersectionality" includes the notion of revision, we comprehend this approach as aligned with and committed to the mission of intersectional justice. With Anna Carastathis this could be phrased as "intersectionality-as-challenge", as a way to "grapple with and overcome our entrenched perceptual-cognitive habits of essentialism, categorial purity, and segregation" (2016: 4). In other words, with this publication, we want to step back and probe different "ways of seeing"—to borrow art critic John Berger's (1977) famous formulation—and propose a revisiting and revising of intersectionality through a focus on visuality and vice versa.

To start off this transdisciplinary enquiry, in the following chapter Magdalena Nowicka asks where difference begins. She engages with conceptual responses to how bodies are categorised by drawing on cognitive, psychological, and philosophical interrogations of classification and the potential discriminatory social outcomes these might have, incorporating empirical samples. In Chap. 4, Elahe Haschemi Yekani links intersectionality research and visual culture studies to enquire into the various ends of visibility. She problematises notions of difference that rely on a binary of invisibility and visibility and discusses "other modes of seeing" in artistic practice and digital media, but also considers how visuality exceeds the realm of representation and accordingly interrogates other "modes of being". Together, these two longer chapters deal with the perception and possible intersectional reimaginations of difference. Here our disciplinary trainings as well as our individual research foci differ somewhat in geopolitical orientation. While Nowicka works on migration and race focusing particularly on Central and Eastern Europe, Haschemi Yekani is concerned with postcolonial and diasporic Anglophone cultural expressions and artistic practice. This obviously also has an impact on our respective perspectives and their limitations. A unifying principle underlying these chapters is the discussion of multiple shorter vignettes to demonstrate the various productive inroads into an intersectional engagement with visuality and a rethinking of intersectionality through visuality.

The research that made this publication possible was generously funded by the Volkswagen Foundation within an initiative called "Original—isn't it?", "Originalitätsverdacht" in German. This line of funding is explicitly intended to support transdisciplinary collaborative research that is based on a suspicion, or a hunch, rather than on already established concepts. This format more than anything gave us time and space to engage with theoretical approaches that might not be at the heart of our individual disciplinary traditions. Accordingly, this book, which results from joint readings, discussions amongst the three authors and invited guests and colleagues as well as the engagement with various visual materials, should not be understood as one unanimous or authoritative perspective on how research on visuality and intersectionality should be best combined. Indeed, we think that a spectrum of different, at times conflicting, points of view is an unavoidable and necessary aspect of any transdisciplinary dialogue.

In the preparation for this book, we had the great privilege to work with several colleagues and artists in a format that we called "conversations" which took place in Berlin at the DeZIM-Institute and the venue Südblock in the second half of 2019 and whose programme was curated by Tiara Roxanne, an academic and artist who specialises in performance and Artificial Intelligence, who collaborated with us on the project from its inception. This open conversation format invited guests to reflect on films, texts, and performance and functioned as a way of combining intersectionality with methods that might be more strongly associated with artistic research. These contributions are reflected in the text by Roxanne (Chap. 3) which is positioned between the two longer articles from our sociological and cultural studies standpoints and it presents some methodological and disciplinary reflections undergirding our overall conversation in this book. Consequently, with this publication we do not present one coherent theory or model for an intersectional analysis of visuality. Instead, we invite multiple open-ended inroads into a transdisciplinary revis(ualis)ing of intersectionality.

Notes

1. For genealogies of intersectionality, cf., for example, Carastathis (2016), Carbado et al. (2013), Collins and Bilge (2016), Meyer (2017); cf. also Taylor (2017) on the importance of the Combahee River Collective in this context. Nash (2019) provides an instructive discussion of what she calls "intersectionality wars" (2019) in her revaluation of the contested academic legacy of the term. We follow her caution that while, "To care for intersectionality, then, is to care for black women's intellectual production and to care for black women as knowledge producers, as subjects", we also do not have to limit the concept within a narrowly proprietary framework. Instead, we take Nash's call to "let intersectionality move and transform in unexpected and perhaps challenging ways" (2019: 80) as an inspiration to rethink and reimagine the uses of intersectionality in relation to visuality from our different disciplinary standpoints in this book.
2. In the spirit of visual multiplicity, the authors use various textual means to signify the constructed nature of categories of difference in the following chapters, including capitalisation and italicisation of designations such as "Black" and "*white*" but also words such as "Otherness" might appear both in regular and capitalised spelling. The term trans will also be used followed by an asterisk as trans* as well as without. We have decided to keep these differing spellings—at times motivated by disciplinary conventions—visible in the text rather than opting for a streamlining across chapters.
3. We do not suggest that all forms of discrimination can be reduced to the (mis)recognition of visual difference. Some disabilities as well as sexual preference, for instance, might be considered less visually evident even if they are embodied.
4. To ensure better accessibility the term is spelled without brackets as "revisualising" intersectionality in the title of the book. However, even when printed without brackets, it should be understood as combining the notion of revising and visualising, and we use both spellings revisualising and revis(ualis)ing interchangeably throughout the book.

Works Cited

Berger, John. 1977. *Ways of Seeing. Based on the BBC Television Series with John Berger*. London: British Broadcasting Corporation and Penguin.
Bhaskar, Roy. 1989. *Reclaiming Reality: A Critical Introduction to Contemporary Philosophy*. London: Routledge.
Bilge, Sirma. 2013. Intersectionality Undone. Saving Intersectionality from Feminist Intersectionality Studies. *Du Bois Review* 10 (2): 405–424. https://doi.org/10.1017/S1742058X13000283.
Carastathis, Anna. 2016. *Intersectionality. Origins, Contestations, Horizons*. Lincoln: University of Nebraska Press.
Carbado, Devon W., Kimberlé Williams Crenshaw, Vickie M. Mays, and Barbara Tomlinson. 2013. Intersectionality: Mapping the Movements of a Theory. *Du Bois Review* 10 (2): 303–312. https://doi.org/10.1017/S1742058X13000349.
Cho, Sumi, Kimberlé Williams Crenshaw, and Leslie McCall. 2013. Toward a Field of Intersectionality Studies: Theory, Applications, and Praxis. *Signs* 38 (4): 785–810. https://doi.org/10.1086/669608.
Collins, Patricia Hill. 2019. *Intersectionality as Critical Social Theory*. Durham: Duke University Press.
Collins, Patricia Hill, and Sirma Bilge. 2016. *Intersectionality*. Cambridge: Polity.
Crenshaw, Kimberlé Williams. 1995. Mapping the Margins. Intersectionality, Identity Politics, and Violence Against Women of Color. In *Critical Race Theory: The Key Writings That Formed the Movement*, eds. Kimberlé Williams Crenshaw, Neil Gotanda, Garry Peller, and Kendall Thomas, 357–383. New York: The New Press.
———. 1998. A Black Feminist Critique of Antidiscrimination Law and Politics. In *The Politics of Law. A Progressive Critique*, ed. David Kairys, 356–379. New York: Basic Books.
Lugones, Maria. 1994. Purity, Impurity, and Separation. *Signs* 19 (2): 458–479.
McCall, Leslie. 2005. The Complexity of Intersectionality. *Signs* 30 (3): 1771–1802.
Meyer, Katrin. 2017. *Theorien der Intersektionalität zur Einführung*. Hamburg: Junius.
Mirza, Heidi S. 2013. "A Second Skin": Embodied Intersectionality, Transnationalism and Narratives of Identity and Belonging among Muslim Women in Britain. *Women's Studies International Forum* 36 (3): 5–15. https://doi.org/10.1016/j.wsif.2012.10.012.
Nash, Jennifer C. 2019. *Black Feminism Reimagined after Intersectionality*. Durham: Duke University Press.
Puar, Jasbir K. 2007. *Terrorist Assemblages. Homonationalism in Queer Times*. Durham: Duke University Press.

———. 2012. "I Would Rather Be a Cyborg Than a Goddess": Becoming-Intersectional in Assemblage Theory. *philoSOPHIA: A Journal of Continental Feminism* 2 (1): 49–66.

Rodó-Zárate, Maria, and Marta Jorba. 2020. Metaphors of Intersectionality: Reframing the Debate with a New Proposal. *European Journal of Women's Studies*. https://doi.org/10.1177/1350506820930734.

Rorty, Richard. 1979. *Philosophy and the Mirror of Nature*. Princeton: Princeton University Press.

Taylor, Keeanga-Yamahtta. 2017. *How We Get Free. Black Feminism and the Combahee River Collective*. Chicago: Haymarket Books.

Winker, Gabriele, and Nina Degele. 2011. Intersectionality as Multi-Level Analysis: Dealing with Social Inequality. *European Journal of Women's Studies* 18 (1): 51–66. https://doi.org/10.1177/1350506810386084.

Open Access This chapter is licensed under the terms of the Creative Commons Attribution 4.0 International License (http://creativecommons.org/licenses/by/4.0/), which permits use, sharing, adaptation, distribution and reproduction in any medium or format, as long as you give appropriate credit to the original author(s) and the source, provide a link to the Creative Commons licence and indicate if changes were made.

The images or other third party material in this chapter are included in the chapter's Creative Commons licence, unless indicated otherwise in a credit line to the material. If material is not included in the chapter's Creative Commons licence and your intended use is not permitted by statutory regulation or exceeds the permitted use, you will need to obtain permission directly from the copyright holder.

CHAPTER 2

Where Difference Begins

Magdalena Nowicka

Abstract This chapter engages with seeing as a socio-cultural process and asks if it is possible to see beyond established categories. Nowicka illustrates how people struggle to order others into neatly delineated groups related to their gender, sexuality, race, and ethnicity. Drawing on research from cognitive science and philosophy, the chapter investigates how we arrive from a messy sensory visual experience to discrete social categories. Thereby, the central interest of this chapter is the question how we could arrive at categories that better correspond to the intersectional experience of being in the world. Finally, the chapter points to the central role of attention and discusses the significance of the scientific gaze and the potential of artistic enquiry for a more intersectional form of seeing.

Keywords Intersectionality • Perception • Categorising • Stereotyping • Attention

> *We don't see things as they are, we see them as we are*
> —The quote is attributed to the writer Anaïs Nin (1961) but also present in the Talmudic concept of dream analysis and was used since the nineteenth century in multiple popular and scientific writings.

Where does difference begin? How do we (un)know others and their identities when looking at them? How can we learn to rely less on visual evidence? Is it possible to shift our perception of the body as an expression of 'true' and 'essential' difference irrespective of the visual understanding of it? Could we view others intersectionally; can we see them in a way that resembles our own intersectional experience as a body in the world? Addressing these questions in this chapter, I seek to understand how 'seeing' works. How do we arrive from visual clues to discrete categories? To what extent is visual perception moulded by discrete categories? Is there any place for distraction within these processes, and could it help us to see intersectionally?

To answer these questions, I will consult works from various disciplines, mostly in psychology and cognitive science[1] which engage in understanding human perception. Occasionally, I will also refer to works from philosophy and the social sciences. While direct dialogue between the disciplines is sporadic, their findings frequently transgress the boundaries of a singular discipline. For example, cognition researchers investigate how we select the features we perceive, how we judge their similarity and weigh their importance, and how we learn what to attend to and what to ignore. Similar interests were followed by art historians as well, and their observations are equally productive for revis(ualis)ing intersectionality. By combining different disciplinary knowledge on how we perceive and categorise the world, this chapter identifies potentials for intersectional seeing. Rather than examining intersecting oppressions and their structural underpinnings, it probes an intersectional way of seeing others as a mode of engagement with the world which bears the potential for overcoming injustice rooted in sexism, racism, ableism, and classism.

Relying on visual evidence to establish difference is habitual but can become conscious when the context in which categorising by looking happens changes in a way that leaves actors without adequate linguistic and cognitive "tools" to manage the situation. Such disruption and dislocation, referred to as the "hysteresis-effect" (Bourdieu 1977; Strand and Lizardo 2017), is a common experience of many international migrants, but it was described also in the context of rural-urban movements, or for people who are first-generation elites. Two examples from my own research on Polish migrants in England and Germany are illustrative of how people tend to project their own ideas about race, gender, and sexuality onto others who they do not know. Polish migrants struggle to establish what they consider others' 'true nature' and with how to fit them into the categories they are familiar with but which mismatch the current context.

Surfaces

In an interview, Dominik,[2] a 40-year-old father of two, and a migrant from Poland, now living in Munich, Germany, tells us:[3]

> When I see a transvestite, or transsexual person, I don't know, a so-called woman with a beard, this is not a sight that is shocking to me. Sometimes I meet a woman, she is very well-made up but I can see that she has an Adam's apple.

Dominik alludes to the Austrian artist known as Conchita Wurst, who gained international popularity after winning the Eurovision Song Contest in 2014. She established herself as a LGBTQ+ icon. On stage, she often appeared in feminine clothes, with long hair, and a beard. Describing the presence of queer people on the streets in Munich, Dominik tries to "detect" what he perceives to be a person's "true gender" and detach it from what he calls "their performance" and suggests he can indeed establish it just by looking.

Dominik does not personally know any "transsexual people, or any transvestites", as he says. But seeing a person, he projects his imagination of masculinity and femininity, gained through socialisation in Poland, onto them. Bech's (2014) notion of "surface" is useful to analyse the narratives such as those produced by Dominik. "Surface" expresses how masculinities and femininities are constructed in the process of looking at others—strangers—in urban public spaces. As urban encounters are superficial and fleeting, it is the "surface" of the other—aestheticised and sexualised, ethnicised and racialised—which becomes the subject of evaluation. The observer seems to stabilise the observed through their gaze and looks at them analytically as though this person would exist in some accessible state available for comparison and judgement (Crary 1999: 300).

Anita, a Polish born Londoner, an entry-level office worker and social mother to her partner's biological son,[4] gives an example of what she considers to be "typically British femininity":

> Recently, I just didn't know what to do anymore. A woman came [to school] wearing a pink tracksuit. With that topknot on her head, flip-flops, and a

sign spelling 'VIP girl', right? I am thinking: Woman, you have a child, you are not a girl anymore, you are a woman. Sometimes I really feel the itch to come up to them and [she makes a strong shaking motion], fuck, get a grip, really. (Lisiak 2017: 47)

Anita's narration reveals her disgust turning into anger in the situation that seems irreconcilable with the norms she knows from home, and the class, ethnic, and gender prejudice she harbours. But this quotation is interesting mostly because it demonstrates that just by looking at another woman, Anita thinks she can establish who she is: here, English, white and working class. Her subjective optical impression becomes a kind of 'objective, shared truth'.

Both Dominik and Anita are fixated on perceived visual differences between themselves and the others, and between the 'norm' and the 'aberration'. As looking at others is relational, the gendered or ethnicised difference is constructed in relation to other white men and women. In all interviews, when Polish women talk about people of colour or Muslims, they always mention their ethnicity or religion (Lisiak 2017: 50); when men speak of other men and women's sexuality that is non-heteronormative, they refer implicitly to white Germans or white English people. Conversely, Muslim men are denied queer sexuality (Wojnicka and Nowicka 2021).

These narrations are instructive for at least two intertwined reasons. First, when projecting their ideas around gender, sexuality, ethnicity, and race on the bodies of others, the interviewees categorise others as members of some groups, such as German, British, straight or queer, men or women. They do so by placing some selected features of other people's appearance and performance in focus and by ignoring others. Second, attending to some and ignoring other differences is not accidental. Attending to difference and ignoring difference reflects and enacts power. As Wojnicka and Nowicka (2021) and Lisiak (2017) explicate, Polish migrants in England and in Germany do not hesitate to demonstrate dismissive and discriminatory opinions of Muslim men and women as the racialisation and stigmatisation of Muslim bodies is largely legitimised in public discourses in these countries, as well as in Poland, which remains an important point of reference for these migrants. For Polish women in England and Germany, depicted by Lisiak (2017), *white* female bodies are visible, as they are also valuable, while non-white and Muslim bodies are invisible and misrecognised. What is also invisible, in the sense of not being addressed consciously, is the bodies' whiteness (Ahmed 2007), for whiteness is the norm in these countries. Aligning with the first and devaluating the second, Polish women signal their belonging to the white hegemonic group. Those who, like Anita, stress their distance to British women, try to overcome their experience of downward class mobility by contrasting their education and civility to the perceived lack of it amongst lower-class British women who inhabit the same neighbourhoods in London or Birmingham and where the Polish migrant women do not feel they really belong.

Similarly, Polish men in Germany described by Wojnicka and Nowicka (2021) establish a proximity to German men and distance themselves from Muslim men if they read them as heterosexual. But they also distance themselves from German men by questioning their "masculine" features: in the narrations we collected, German masculinity is presented as "harmless" or even "too civilised", tamed, having some "feminine" features. German men are portrayed as paying exaggerated attention to their looks and avoiding physical confrontation. Furthermore, they are seen by Polish men as not chivalrous enough, and thus lacking respect towards women and vulnerable people. Polish masculinity emerges here as a golden middle between an "aggressive Muslim" and "feminised German" male other.

A Third Race

Barbara, a Polish born middle-aged mother of two who lives in a mid-sized town in the Midlands, UK, interviewed in 2011[5] tells me about the relations between Polish migrants in England and other nationals. She gives examples of some minor tensions between English and Polish people and then says:

> I know such stories that they [English] don't like us [Polish] but I think if that many different nationalities would come to Poland, like it is in England, I don't think it would go well. Polish people don't like Kurdish, Bangladeshi, as they [Poles] say ciapaty, or how else they call them? Dirty, ciapaci. That's what they say.

She distances herself from this term and adds quickly "for me all are humans" but later in the interview she mentions that some of her Polish (former) friends who turned her down because she "married a *ciapaty*" (cf. Fiałkowska 2018), and she accepts this term as describing her own husband.

Another Polish woman, Anna, interviewed in 2011 in the same town, manager in a shop, in her twenties, recalls her first days in England and how she tried to find accommodation. She replied to an ad in a newspaper and went, accompanied by her friend, to meet the potential landlord:

> There came a guy, just imagine, with a car, ciapaty and [said to us] come here my girls, come quickly, get into the car, get in! And I say no, our luggage is here. And he continues, get in and takes my friend's hand, tries to draw her into his car... I got scared, he could kidnap us.

She goes on describing how she and her friend could free themselves from the man and how she feared him. I asked her to explain what she means by '*ciapaty*' and she explains: "you know, all kinds of nationalities, all Indians, I don't know". A similar explanation was given to me in an interview in 2011 by Bianka and her partner, both in their mid-twenties. She works as a picker and packer in a large warehouse in the Midlands; he is a truck driver. Both say, "We have no negative feelings towards... Indians, *ciapaci*" and Bianka clarifies for me:

> In general, in England, I think I've heard it for the first time in Coventry, this is a term describing a person who is not black and not white, who is in-between, it means it denotes an Indian, Algerian, Tunisian, or those from Middle East for example... those whose skin colour is not terribly dark. Funny, because....

I interrupt her to ask who uses this term. She continues: "Polish people in England... The first thing we learnt here [in England] was 'oh, here comes *ciapaty*'" and her partner adds:

> I don't know, I thought that ciapaty is a strange colour, such undefined [...] and the best thing is that ciabatta[6] is simple a kind of their bread, so perhaps that is where it comes from?

They go on pondering the term and cannot decide whether the term denotes Indian and other people who eat chapatis frequently, or whether the term denotes, as they say, their "undefined" skin colour. Notwithstanding the original intention, this neologism is used by Poles in England to represent mostly South Asians but also people from the Middle East (cf. Gawlewicz 2015). It is hardly surprising that Poles seek a new term—a category—to describe people they encounter and people who do not fit into their imaginary of racialised distinction. Public discourse on race and racism in Poland focuses only on Black people; respectively it creates a white-black binary. In the British context, this understanding of racial categories is altered and extended by a 'third race' defined by their unspecified skin colour (Nowicka 2018). The lexical analysis of the interviews showed that the various labels depicting 'Indian' are clustered with the labels 'white' and 'black', and thus belong to a racial classification scheme. The narrations around people of a 'third race' often include negative stereotypes that function within a racialised hierarchy, as this quotation[7] demonstrates:

> [...] they [Indians] are like this, they are different, for me worse, but at least not aggressive. They have less aggression in them than blacks who come from Africa. Because I don't speak of blacks born in Europe, they have a different attitude, but those immigrants from Africa, Somalia, their life is a computer game, you can kill, and the person will be reborn. This is their attitude. The lives of others do not mean anything to them. (Nowicka 2018: 831)

And another participant adds:

> [...] it does not disturb me if a person is black if this black person is nice, educated, intelligent, smart and resourceful, well organised and so on, and not every black is lazy, inane, arrogant, impolite, but I simply have exactly such black colleagues; India, this is such a nation that is convinced they have to get everything for free and others ought to work for them. The English got into this trouble, forget the blacks but those Indians, Muslim, they all flood this place [...]. (Nowicka 2018: 831)

As Shimada (2007: 114) notices, "the gaze at the other culture is fixed long before the encounter". So are the Polish migrants' narrations about people they encounter in England's cities moulded by understandings of racialised others that function in Poland (Strani and Szczepaniak-Kozak 2018; Adamczak-Krysztofowicz and Szczepaniak-Kozak 2017). Yet studying Polish migrants in England over time allows us also to observe how their racial vocabularies and attitudes transform within the British social context. When I interviewed Bianka in 2011, she told me she must remember not to use the word *ciapaty* but Indian instead; she signalled her awareness that the term is pejorative and improper although this does not make her change her mind about these people and assigning them, irrespectively of their religious, gendered, and class heterogeneity, to a group of *ciapaty*. In the later interviews (2014–2018), the term *ciapaty* appears seldom but racialist stereotypes about Indian, Pakistani, Bangladeshi, and other groups are frequent in the narrations. They are particularly frequent in Birmingham, and less so in London. A similar 'third race' category is absent from narrations by Polish migrants in Munich and Berlin in Germany (Nowicka and Krzyżowski 2017) which points to the meaning of local racial hierarchies and how they shape migrants' acquisition of cultural codes. Similarly, Poles in the UK use 'Asian' to describe people from South-East Asia even though in Poland 'Asian' refers to Japanese, Chinese and Koreans, primarily. The same, 'Polish-like' understanding of 'Asians' occurs among Polish migrants in Germany.

How the interview participants see others is thus deeply embedded it the racialised cultures in which the Polish migrants function. Coming from a culture where race is perceived as binary, they struggle to establish how to classify those whose skin pigmentation is, in their eyes, neither white nor black. Lacking the knowledge on how to recognise people of Indian, Bangladeshi or other origins, yet sensing the need for racial classification in Britain, they invent 'a third race' as a category based on their visual experience. As this category is linked to mostly negative stereotypes, it becomes also an instrument of power and helps Poles establish social proximity to the white British majority (Fox and Mogilnicka 2019).

The narrations including the neologism *ciapaty* are also a useful example of racial othering within a culture of (visual) essentialism and racialised binaries. This is not to say that Indian, Pakistani, or Kurdish people are 'ambiguous' because of their skin pigmentation but that Poles perceiving their bodies feel 'lost' as they do not neatly fit their idea of two essentially different, thus separate, 'races'. The presence of bodies that do not fit into a pre-imagined category shakes the general psychological essentialism (Medin and Ortony 1989).

In the western hemisphere, more and more people apparently are perceived as not easily classifiable into a white-black racial scheme.[8] Multiracial people appear ambiguous only when racial classification is arbitrary, dichotomous and binary, an 'either-or' question. The presence of so-called multiracial or mixed-race people do not fit official monoracial classifications such as the national Censuses (Aspinall and Song 2014) or the social scientific understanding of visible minorities constructed through their difference from the white majority (Song 2020). This has also resulted in a new branch of psychological experimental research which tries to understand how people make categorisations of multiracial individuals, depending on their own racial identity, degree of exposure to multiracial people, and the social context of the encounters (Chen and Hamilton 2012; Freeman et al. 2013, 2016; Lamer et al. 2018). Generally, those outside a particular group might disregard the internal heterogeneity of a group: for example, people who do not identify as multiracial may assign people to a general category 'black' while its members may have a differentiated identity as mixed-race people (Feliciano 2015). Monoracial, in particular white people, are more likely to miscategorise those who are multiracial (Herman 2010). Research shows that people who are 'racially ambiguous' experience different forms of discrimination; they are more likely to be stigmatised (Grier et al. 2014) in institutional contexts such as within the criminal justice system (MacLin and Malpass 2001). They may be rejected by monoracial white and Black groups simultaneously (Campion 2019; Khanna 2010; Ali 2003; Song 2017; Chaney et al. 2020).

Others are therefore treated as surfaces reflecting one's own classification schemes and stereotypes. This process is not accidental but deeply rooted in one's cultural repertoire which governs which aspects of someone's appearance is foregrounded: it could be gender, or someone's light or dark skin pigmentation, body shape and bodily movements, or other features (Nowicka 2018). For example, to white Polish migrants, whiteness of others is a norm, something obvious and therefore backgrounded, whilst the stereotyping of Muslim men as patriarchs, machos, or 'pashas' makes Polish migrants dismiss the possibility of their queerness. Clearly, such categorisations are flawed and errant and often misunderstand the self-identifications of others. They are embedded in social structures of power and reflect them. Disavowing physical attractiveness when describing lower class or Black women, Polish white female migrants position themselves in a racialised hierarchy in today's Britain and signal their aspiration to belong to the white middle class. Importantly for our book, these examples demonstrate how such positionalities rely on seeing and being seen. And, even more importantly, the study of Polish migrants tells us also that not only how we see others (stereotypes) but also, *what* we see in others (perception) can change when confronted with unfamiliar circumstances.

The Power of Seeing

Social sciences make it clear that we live in a world in which our chances of being and becoming are largely structured by how other people see us. For example, it is well documented that women wearing headscarves experience discrimination in hiring processes (Leckcivilize and Straub 2018), obese applicants receive fewer call-backs for job interviews (Rooth 2010), and people perceived as more attractive and beautiful tend to earn more (Parrett 2015; Doorley and Sierminska 2015). Science also relies on appearance: migration scholarship, for example, frequently addresses people of colour as 'visibly non-white' minorities (Song 2020), using visible appearance as a marker of racial identity. Part of medical and epidemiological research routinely employs classifications referring to appearance and thereby perpetuates and stabilises racism (Hunt and Megyesi 2008; Beaudevin and Schramm 2019).

As Kress and van Leeuwen (1996: 168) write, "seeing has, in our culture, become synonymous with understanding [...]. The world 'as we see it' [...] has become the measure for what is 'real' and 'true'". Thus, we ignore that the world we feel to be real becomes so only through "the continual recurrence of identical, familiar, related things in their logicized character" (Nietzsche 1968: §569). Yet the ways we are seen do not do justice to us, in many ways. People suffer when some of their features which, to them, are vital to their identity are overlooked by others; or when they are reduced to only a few characteristics and the complexity of their personality or positionality remains unrecognised. 'Looking' in all its different forms and modulations can be a powerful tool with which to build or sustain privilege and exclude particular individuals, or indeed, entire groups (Brighenti 2010). Being an object of another's gaze defines the lived experience of people "locked" in such reification (Fanon 1986: 89ff). On the other hand, some groups may use the visibility of some aspects of their identity or positionality tactically, for example in the political struggle for recognition (Spivak 1988; Narayan 1997). When and if strategic (visual) essentialism is legitimate is a subject of controversial debates (Pande 2017; Stone 2004; Hoyt et al. 2019).

How we are seen is not exactly who we are or want to be. Divergences between self-perception and other's classifications are well documented in the literature on race relations. They may emerge due to different cultural conceptions of a category; for example, 'black' in the US-American, British, or Brazilian context may be understood differently and associated with different features. Also, general and scientific beliefs of race may diverge (Suyemoto et al. 2020). Similarly, the Western popular concepts of gender as a binary, commonly associated with physical characteristics of bodies, is at odds with a scientific, more nuanced, understanding of sex as a spectrum (Ainsworth 2015) as well as with non-Western knowledges (Johnston 2005). There is also historical evidence that boundaries between categories such as *white* and Black vary across time and space. In his influential book *How the Irish Became White*, the historian Noel Ignatiev (1995) describes how Catholics from Ireland who immigrated to the US in the nineteenth century where subjected to discrimination, not dissimilar from that experienced by the Black population there; initially, they also identified with African Americans, but with the changing demographic and political situation in the US, they slowly gained the privileges, rights, and duties of white Americans. Similarly, Eastern European migrants in the west of Europe struggle to gain recognition while their *whiteness* is under scrutiny (Tereshchenko et al. 2019; Paraschivescu 2020; Fox et al. 2015). These examples demonstrate that *whiteness* or Blackness encapsulates more than just skin colour; it reflects a complex system of privilege and disadvantage which emerges and develops in particular historical and geographical contexts. But these illustrations also show that social visibility as a racialised other is embedded in particular contexts and political, social, and technological arrangements (Brighenti 2010; Song 2020). For example, whether someone is considered Black or poor can depend on where the encounter takes place. Recently, Ludwig and Kraus (2019) demonstrated that some features of a neighbourhood, such as degree of ethnic diversity or wealth, may impact people's judgements on other's and their lives. This means that people are read through the contexts in which they appear. Visibility is thus an outcome of a complex social process which locates people in particular relational positions (Anthias 2008).

In this sense, social relations are inscribed on bodies. Despite the fact that historians of race relations (as discussed above) could convincingly demonstrate the historical and geographical variation of social categories, this knowledge is somehow contradictory to the "western modern imaginary" (Taylor 2007) which makes us believe that the body is the expression of the subject's "psychic interior" (Grosz 1993: 198). It means that 'race' or 'gender' is *seen* as biological (natural) difference and not merely a projection of social relations on bodies, or embodied social relations. Our eyes and our brain seem just to 'reflect' the 'true' nature of the bodies they encounter. Seeing is believed to be an act of 'absorbing' existing human difference. Oyěwùmí (1997) reminds us that privileging biological explanations of differences of race, gender, or class is historically new and geographically limited to European cultures. Other cultures do not privilege the visual in the same way. The reliance on seeing as the direct path to knowing is thus a typically western mode of understanding. As infants in western modern culture are asymmetrically exposed to different types of faces, including female, male and other genders, and more to their own-race than other-race (Anzures et al. 2010; Quinn et al. 2018), children by the age of three to five develop racial biases (Gelman 2003; Hirschfeld 1996). Accordingly, this racialised way of seeing is perpetuated intergenerationally.

Race and gender seem to be known by observable physical cues that inhere in bodies and they seem to be experienced unmediated by culture, that is, they gain their salience from their self-evidently striking nature (Obasogie 2010: 586). They are social categories that have a strong visual character and tend to be essentialised (Bastian and Haslam 2007). Yet, the visuality of race and gender is not limited to immediate visual perception of the observer. The imaginary of race and gender as visually perceptible and discrete categories is also linguistically anchored (Orians 2018). Visual metaphors are common in our languages: we look at a problem, we see the point, adopt a viewpoint, focus on an issue, and see things in a perspective (Kress and van Leeuwen 1996: 168). Such metaphors link semantic representations and cognitive structures (Wilson and Foglia 2017) and affect how we act (Lakoff 2014). By visual language, even blind people learn that race is a matter of visible features, and they learn how to align their sensory experience of others to the visual racial scheme (Obasogie 2014).

Intersectional Perspectives

Being in the world and experiencing it both mentally and corporeally means, that we think, feel, and behave in complex ways which can hardly be articulated in words. The language which we have at our disposal to make sense of this experience, as humans and as social scientists, relies heavily on discrete social concepts such as 'woman', 'short', 'person of colour', 'student', 'mother', 'transgender'.

The terms I could use to describe myself are of a different nature. Some relate to my social role—mother, researcher. And some refer to my appearance—for example, short. I identify as a woman, and most people identify me as a cis-woman after assessing the shape of my body, the timbre of my voice, and the way in which I dress which they associate with femininity. I am below average height for women in Germany, but of average height in Japan. Whether I am always white, is another complex story (Fox et al. 2012; Böröcz and Sarkar 2017; Bonnett 1998). As a person born in Eastern Europe, my whiteness in present-day Western Europe may be contested (Lapiņa and Vertelytė 2020). Thus, being white or short is relative to the context in which I live.

I can say that my experience is that of a rather short, white woman who is a mother and researcher, but this does not capture fully how I experience the world. Moreover, some of these categories are highly political, and if I describe myself as white, this is not just an indication that my skin pigmentation is rather light but could be understood as an expression of a political identity. As whiteness for so long has been the unacknowledged norm because of white supremacy, if I do not articulate that I am white, my counterpart might assume it. Nevertheless, by acknowledging the intersection of these categories, I can try to express that being white inflects my being a woman, to claim simply that I am a woman, denies the particular experience of white womanhood and how it affects 'being a woman'. Or, in other words, there are many parts of my identity that are reliant on others: my experience of 'being a woman' is influenced by the fact that I am a mother; my experience of motherhood is influenced by the fact that I am white and so on. These parts of me are inextricably linked and cannot simply be separated and observed side-by-side. I need to establish a conceptual relationship (Avargues-Weber and Giurfa 2015: 3) between these categories to describe myself in an intersectional way.

Yet even the intersections of categories do not fully capture the complexity of experience, for each category tends to be too large or too narrow. One can be a woman in a myriad of ways, and white or black in a myriad of ways as well. It is the intra-categorical heterogeneity which challenges the oversimplified description of human experience. While it seems obvious that being a woman, or being white, or being a mother, or heterosexual is multidimensional, assigning something or someone to a category means to suppress the difference within this category and exacerbate its difference from other 'categories' in this topological 'regional' thinking (Jraissati 2019; Mol and Law 1994). Therefore, categories are always contested, and their boundaries and meanings are re-negotiated. But some categories seem more persistent, as they rely on visual evidence—I would probably be perceived as a white woman anywhere but hardly anyone recognises me as a researcher based on my appearance alone.

Intersectionality research gives us a good sense of how the experience of discrimination is irreducible to the workings of one category. As Patricia Hill Collins (2019) argues, intersectionality has always put relationality in focus. The relationality of categories could be understood in a cumulative way, in which one category is added to another, altering the meaning of both (Collins 2019: 229). Relational thinking could also be defined in terms of articulation, juncture, or connection from which two entities create (for a time) a new entity, quality, or pattern. Racism, sexism, capitalism, and homophobia are articulated differently in and across varying social contexts but under certain circumstances they cohere (Collins 2019: 233; Hall 2017). Co-formation as a third type of relational intersectional thinking "seemingly dissolves the categories themselves" (Collins 2019: 241), thereby Collins stresses that this kind of dissolvement is an intellectual and theoretical exercise enabling the development of a holistic analytical framework, for in reality, categories do not dissolve. The aim of intersectional analysis through co-formation is to adequately acknowledge the complexity and irreducibility of the experience in the world, thereby intersectionality research must resist the western modern mode of producing scientific knowledge through dissecting and disaggregating phenomena it studies (Collins 2019: 244).

Collins warns that relationality understood as addition bears the danger of adding categories of experience to each other instead of incorporating a category of analysis into the study (Collins 2019: 227–228). The first move corresponds with what she calls the western logic of segregation. The second means to address how one category is changed when it is added to another. For example, an analysis that starts with gender and 'adds' race and moves to include sexuality, ability, and so on engages with social experience differently than if 'race' or 'ability' are a starting point. The remainders of this chapter involve insights from cognitive science to discuss the possibilities of intersectional categorisation that could account for relationality and fluidity of human experience and identity.

This chapter focuses on race and gender as categories of experience. The decision to exclude class, despite the fact that class is—next to race and gender—a central concept in intersectionality research, in particular in the Marxist tradition of conceptualising race relations, is motivated by several considerations, some conceptual, and some pragmatic. Class designates both one's social and economic position, and an aesthetic and affective disposition (Bourdieu 1984, 1977). An understanding of class includes hierarchical categories of wealth, education, occupational profile, and lifestyle. At the same time, class is an analytical or a descriptive concept used to analyse capitalism and its workings or to describe identities. Visual indicators of wealth, occupation, and education (signalled by lifestyle, clothing, etc.) serve to signal one's social proximity or distance to others. Next to institutionalised forms, this form of distinction is used to exclude members of other classes and secure one's own status and privileged access to resources. Class distinction intersects with gender and race; yet it is also widely believed that people can be mobile across the class hierarchy (Varnum 2013). Indeed, the concept of a middle class is based on the potential class mobility—aspiration of its members to move upwards, and their fears of downward mobility characterise the middle class. In particular, intergenerational class mobility makes the category of class appear more 'social' and less 'biological' or 'genetic' (Kraus and Tan 2015).

While actual class positions continue to structure social relations, and people's visual perceptions of others (Harrits and Pedersen 2018), Collins (2019: 230) argues that class is an underlying master concept (and not a category) for any intersectional research. Adding class to an analysis of gendered and racialised processes and interactions is in fact unnecessary, for class analysis—respectively the analysis of capitalism—must instead prefigure intersectional analyses.

Do We See What Is There?

Current research in cognitive science suggests that categorisation is a basic form of interaction between humans and their environment. Research in the field of neuropsychology, cognitive science, and psychology shows that the world we see is not equivalent to the physical world but 'biased' (in a predisposed way) according to our individual sensorial abilities, such as contrast sensitivity or colour and motion perception, and sensory experiences. The most obvious examples include various forms of colour blindness, or different forms of impairment of perception of depth and three-dimensional structures. But our perception is 'biased' also in other ways which are more relevant in the context of our book.

To clarify, it is useful to distinguish between perception and cognition. Broadly speaking, perception is what puts us in contact with our present surrounding by 'analysing' sensory experiences, while cognition is what enables us to form beliefs, make decisions, to act. There is a discussion in psychology on the extent to which perception is penetrated by our cognition (Firestone and Scholl 2016; Halford and Hine 2016; Montemayor and Haladjian 2017; Vetter and Newen 2014). The research on perception in space, for example in complex multidimensional settings such as a street crossing, shows that cognitive mechanisms may guide our perception; we are attentive to some but ignore other visual stimuli, which is a cognitive effort (Niv et al. 2015). Research on infants proves, on the other hand, that perception of colours as distinct from each other (categorical perception) emerges before infants begin to develop concepts of colour (Franklin 2016), suggesting that perception is indeed separate from cognition. There is further evidence to suggest that the time between seeing and categorising colour or shape is extremely short; it allows for the conclusion that a distinction between perceiving and cognitively categorising an object is not straightforward (Cichy et al. 2014). Ultimately, scholars have come to agree that the demarcation between perception and cognition might be blurry.

The interest in perception is by no means an exclusive domain of cognitive science and psychology. The idea that our perception is not always veridical—a true representation of physical reality—has also been taken up in philosophy (Crane and French 2017). The question philosophers ask is how do we make judgements and form beliefs about the external world? Is there a reality that is completely independent of our thinking? Do we perceive or experience reality directly, or indirectly (through 'the veil'), and thus cannot know what 'true reality' is? Is the nature of perception different from the nature of thought (cognition)? The answers to these questions have epistemological consequences in at least two ways: first, if we, humans, all perceive objects similarly (providing no neurological differences) and independently of our thinking, then we should indeed easily agree on what we see, for we all see the same; secondly, if perception is independent of our beliefs, our perceptual experiences can be seen as a cause and as justification of these beliefs (Smithies 2016). Deroy (2013) gives a simple example: if an apple we see is red and our perception of colour is independent of our thinking, then if one person sees this apple as yellow, then the difference in perception must be due to the person's neurological condition. The rest of us will easily agree that the apple is red. Moreover, our belief that most apples are red is determined by our perceptions of apples as red. Yet various experiments confirm that having learnt that apples are red, and bananas yellow, we are more likely to perceive shapes resembling apples as being red and banana-like shapes as being yellow. Our idea of red apples thus influences our visual perception.

How Do We See What We See?

Cognition is largely about categorisation (Harnad 2017). Categorisation is a mental operation by which the brain classifies objects and events (Cohen and Lefebvre 2017: 2). Any category includes kinds of objects; a category has both an extension (the set of things that are members of that category) and intension (the feature that makes things members of the category rather than another category). From an ontological point of view, all things are members of an infinite number of different categories, and each of their properties/features and their combination is a potential basis (affordance) for assigning the thing to still more categories—(Harnad 2017: 31)—I call this "ontological" intersectionality which is distinct from heterogeneity within one single category.

Recognition is a form of interaction with things. Unlike sensory interaction (through seeing, hearing, smelling, tasting, touching) or naming and describing things—recognising things means to see something as a kind of thing that we have never seen before—that is, as a member of a category. To recognise, we need to abstract, that is to single out some subset of sensory (e.g., visual) input, and ignore the rest (Harnad 2017: 34). To abstract means to detect recurrences *and* to ignore the uniqueness of things and the particularity of their contexts. Through abstraction, we recognise sameness or similarity, and identify *kinds* of objects, states, events, or individuals.

We abstract things that have properties, meaning the features of sensory input that we can detect selectively (Harnad 2017: 36). The interactional approach, following Gibson (1979) conceives of such properties as not simply features of a thing but rather 'affordances', that is "the ways in which things come into the immediate presence of perceivers, not as objects-in-themselves, closed in and contained, but in their potential for the continuation of a form of life" (Ingold 2018: 39). With her proposal for the metaphysics of categories, the philosopher Ásta (2018) argues in a similar manner. She assumes that objects have various physical properties (physical facts); according to Ásta, these are of two kinds: conferred and unconferred. Some (base) properties of an entity may remain unconferred by our judgements. But if we make a judgement on the property, we confer it. This means the entity gains a particular meaning in a specific sociocultural context in how it is conferred by others. Some properties are obviously recognisable as conferred, for example a person's "popularity" is clearly 'not natural' but dependent on a relation someone or something has to other people (Ásta 2018: 8) but other properties seem more 'natural' and unconferred, while they, in fact, are not. Gender or race could be such seemingly unconferred, but in fact conferred, properties.

The cognitive process includes two different operations, discrimination and categorisation (Harnad 2017: 38). Ontological intersectionality can be understood as a spectrum of (visual) impulses. We 'discriminate' between grades through direct comparison, so that we can decide on similarity and dissimilarity of things when we see them (just-noticeable-difference). 'Categorising' means to decide on (dis)similarity of two things in isolation, it is to identify something as bigger or smaller, lighter or darker, based on our memory of the other thing. It means, we need to have a concept of something to categorise what we see (Jraissati 2019: 423). The human capacity to categorise stands in relation to memory capacity and is thus limited (Cowan 2015); in consequence, we categorise things which are very different from one another better (more correctly). This recognition is of importance when we consider 'biased perception', for example, 'racial perception'.

Categorising is a learning process. It includes mapping sensations (received by our senses) onto conceptual spaces (Jraissati 2019). As we learn to categorise things, we also learn to exclude the alternatives, that is what does not belong to a particular conceptual space. If 'affordances' of things are obvious, such as the difference between a floor and a wall, learning how to categorise two surfaces might be easy. If 'affordances' are not immediately clear, learning to categorise requires more effort (Harnad 2017: 43). Naming things (language) helps us to categorise (Folstein et al. 2015; Jraissati 2019). This is the role of culture in which we live and which is based on language: it helps us to deal with ambivalences and uncertainty with respect to categorisation. Without culture, categorisation would be based exclusively on sensory and trial-and-error methods, which involve consciousness. Categorising correctly has one consequence, miscategorising another; of this, we must become conscious. Sensory based learning is trial and error, reward and punishment, through which we get better at categorising correctly. We can think of an analogue to a tennis player who learns consciously how to hit a ball the way it passes the net, and how many attempts the player needs to do it (almost always) correctly, before they become unaware of each movement they make. Such learning is less efficient—in the sense that it takes more time to change the practice—than learning with the help of culture which 'tells us' who is who and how to assign a person to a category making 'fewer mistakes'.

Experiments increasing consciousness might, therefore, not only be ineffective in reducing racial prejudice but even increase it, as long as they happen within a racialised culture (Strick et al. 2015). At the same time, as language impacts visual perception (Jraissati 2019), it is possible that in cultures with language including, for example, a separate word for multiracial individuals, these people are less likely to be miscategorised.

A small number of categories could not function without grounding them in sensory experience; other categories function through association, or, in other words, they acquire their meaning through reference to other categories. 'Race' is such a category which is independent of us seeing differences in humans. The variation within 'racial' groups is greater than it is between them (Witherspoon et al. 2007) as common phenotypic markers exist on a continuum. In this sense, there is no physical or biological difference between 'races'. When we categorise people as belonging to a racial group, we do it with reference/association to several other categories which are grounded in sensory experience such as skin pigmentation, hair texture, eye shape. The closer an 'associative category' is to something that we can directly perceive with the senses, the more concrete, real it seems to us (Vincent-Lamarre et al. 2016: 650). This feeling of being 'true' because something is grounded in the sensory experience can be strengthened through emotions (Kousta et al. 2011).

SEEING THROUGH CULTURE

Recognising human difference depends on various socio-cultural factors, which is well documented for the so called 'other-race' or 'cross-race' effect.[9] It is a socio-cognitive phenomenon which means that people more easily recognise faces of those who belong to their own 'racial group' (Young et al. 2012). It is not quite clear why this is; limited experience could be responsible for this effect (Rhodes et al. 2010). Infants recognise human faces differently depending on their gender (Ramsey et al. 2005) and 'racial characteristics', and this seems to be due to children's asymmetric exposure to people visually different from their parents (Slone et al. 2000; Lee et al. 2017). It is also known that if adults are accustomed to seeing people whose racial identities differ from their own, they are more likely to recognise the face of an 'other-race' person quicker and better (Levin 2000; Walker and Hewstone 2006). If someone is socialised with people whose identity is similar to their own, the 'cross-race' effect could be supported by the frequency or repetition of information (Kahneman and Tversky 1972). Thereby both gender and 'race' seem to matter at the same time. Masculine and feminine faces, for example, attract our attention differently quickly and for a different period of time; also, women tend to attend to 'own-race' women longer (Lovén et al. 2012). There is some evidence that those who harbour racial prejudices are slower when it comes to recognising the faces of people whose 'race' is different from their own (Costandi 2012); reducing prejudice could minimise the 'cross-race' effect. Also, we tend to see people who belong to a group to which we also count ourselves as more heterogeneous than members of an out-group (Meissner and Brigham 2001).

As previously mentioned, categorisation relies on suppressing difference within and exaggerating the difference between people to enable the construction of groups. Following Searle's (1996) account of the construction of social reality, we can say that in the process of categorisation, somebody becomes what they were not before: through culture, a body becomes a racialised or gendered, young or old, abled or disabled body; skin becomes white or black; the shape of nose or eyes becomes a marker of belonging to a group.

For a long time, psychology maintained that categorisation necessarily results in stereotyping. Stereotyping is linking additional information to a category. As both processes—categorisation and stereotyping—are largely implicit and include oversimplification, it was difficult to prove their distinctive nature. But newer research suggests that these two processes might be independent though interrelated (Ito and Tomelleri 2017). It seems that categorisation results in stereotyping only upon the existence of other enabling circumstances. A popular account says that stereotypes deviate from the 'true' or 'real' features of the person or a group. Stereotyping is 'easier' if it focuses on the most different or ample type from a group, one that represents it best. It thus is also easier when difference is expressed as a binary contrast, for example black and white. Stereotypes 'anchor' better on such most highlighted types.

Stereotyping could also be understood as the idealisation of a category: for example, the category 'grandmother' includes people who are female and mothers of a parent; a typical grandmother, though, includes additional information (context-specific), for example: white hair, rocking chair, bakes cookies. If a person's features do not correspond with this stereotype, we might have problems categorising her as 'grandmother' or might miscategorise her. Similarity to the stereotype in this sense provides probabilistic information about the person's membership in the category (Hampton 1998).

Stereotyping could be considered the mechanism which translates categorisation into social hierarchy, particularly if a stereotype is negatively loaded, or when stereotypes lead to largely invalid/assumptive expectations of a person's behaviour. For example, associating women with acts of care and love might result in a gendered expectation of women, casting them as stay-at-home mothers, or limiting their occupational horizons as those engaged largely with care-work. Instead of thinking of stereotypes as a biased idea of people or groups, newest cognitive research more forcefully acknowledges the role of culture, observing that, for example, stereotypes have different cultural value (Hinton 2017). In this sense, a 'biased view' means a view that diverges from the hegemonic position (social norm) rather than from a 'true' condition, quality, or characteristics of a person (or a group, an object, a situation). Stereotypes thus reflect a history of discrimination and domination of some groups over others; racial stereotypes, for example, are rooted in histories of enslavement and geopolitics of exclusion, and gendered stereotypes reflect a long history of male domination (Hernando 2017).

Researchers have been interested in how stereotyping, whether ascribed to people or objects, positive or negative, is an effective tool in rapid decision making (Bordalo et al. 2016). It has been argued that implicit associations have an evolutionary basis and bring about a survival benefit (Fox 1992). This does not mean, of course, that the current content of stereotypes (e.g., on gender or race) is good or necessary, but that stereotyping can be an effective way of dealing with the complexity of the world, a feature that Devine and Sherman (1992) call a 'cognitive economy'. The mechanism used in stereotyping is described by Tversky and Kahneman (Kahneman and Tversky 1972, 1973; Tversky and Kahneman 1974) as representativeness heuristic. Heuristic is a practical method, a 'mental shortcut' used in making rapid decisions and solving problems. The representativeness heuristic relies on assessing similarity of objects and organising them around the category, according to the assumption that like goes with like, and thus causes and effects should also resemble each other. Stereotypes could be thus defined as a human brain strategy for coping with limited information processing capacities in a complex social world.

The question is how to change implicit associations that lead to social injustice, discrimination, and exclusion if the mechanism apart from stereotyping is so central to our being in the world. One way to do it is to try to replace one association in semantic memory with another one. For example, a negative association could be replaced by a positive or neutral one. As this is done through a conscious training, it is less efficient (or cognitively more costly) than unconscious associating, the effects of such trainings are not durable (Lai et al. 2016). Neither explicit reflection on one's own racial privilege (white privilege checking) nor learning of novel associations and erasing of the old ones, proved so far to be an effective way of changing stereotypes (Kalev et al. 2006; Boatright-Horowitz et al. 2012). Yet the content of stereotypes changes over time, albeit slowly, and therefore some researchers suggest that to change stereotypes requires a change of the culture in which a stereotype is embedded.

A more viable possibility is suggested by research on the 'predictive brain'. Clark (2013, 2014) suggests that attention is functional, and that human perception is predicting. The dynamic brain predicts the experience and 'compares' the prediction with reality; if the expectation was incorrect (does not match the reality well), the brain will 'correct' it and predict better next time. To minimise error, the brain uses probability calculations; these are culture specific and expressed as stereotypical knowledge (Hinton 2017). Following this trait, we could speculate that people frequently confronted with unpredicted, surprising occurrences could adapt their stereotypes. Each time their prediction turns out wrong, their brain 'recalculates' and revises the prior prediction to get better next time. This mechanism could be used by artistic research, or arts more generally, to increase the capacity for intersectional seeing.

Towards Intersectional Stereotyping

Intersectionality poses a challenge to prevalent theories of stereotyping. Intersectionality research seeks to contest essentialised and fixed group categories as a mode of understanding our experience in the world; stereotyping is the process of establishing essentialised, exaggerated conceptions of individuals and/or groups. Therefore, the two concepts might be incongruent (Cassese 2019; Remedios and Sanchez 2018). The major problem of research on stereotyping is that it operates within a particular historic and cultural context which prioritises discrete social categories. One result of this is the compartmentalisation of research on prejudice and stereotyping, it is the focus on one domain or category, such as gender or race (Bigler and Liben 2006; Ghavami and Peplau 2013). Some research tries to overcome this limitation by manipulating one category (e.g., gender) while keeping the other constant (e.g., race), and in this way testing intersections of these two categories. Only recently, psychology addressed how stereotyping is complicated by the fact that people belong to multiple social groups simultaneously (Cassese 2019; Petsko and Bodenhausen 2020). This research acknowledges earlier studies which demonstrated that stereotypes of black men in leadership roles may change from negative to positive depending if these men are heterosexual or not (Wilson et al. 2017), or that black individuals are judged more negatively when they are young as opposed to old, which suggested that single-category-based evaluations are contingent on another classification (here, race and age) (Kang and Chasteen 2009).

Yet the problem remains that this research nevertheless relies on a binary gender scheme (male-female) as well as a fixed category of race (usually dual, as white-Black, or triad—white-Black-Asian) irrespective of the context of research and fluid nature of racial distinctions, or the gradual character of skin pigmentation. Moreover, the experiments usually focus on faces, and their results therefore are hardly applicable to real-life situations when people 'reinterpret' the information vis-à-vis information on body shape, clothing, and so on (Remedios and Sanchez 2018). Also, emotions may impact categorisation (Brooks et al. 2018), and thus also intersectional stereotyping. Further, studies frequently manipulate stimuli (such as pictures of different faces) with the help of software which itself might be racially biased (cf. Chap. 4).

Notwithstanding these major shortages of the psychological research on intersectional stereotyping, the debate offers some interesting observations. So far, several possible mechanisms of intersectional stereotyping have been suggested. Firstly, it seems that targeting subjects by stereotypes may proceed by all detectable social identities of the target at once; for example, a person could be detected as 'white young woman' and not as 'white', 'young' and 'woman' and a stereotype would be integrated (Ghavami and Peplau 2013). It presumes though, that a person possesses a premade integrity. Secondly, stereotyping might focus on a certain social identity (possibly because of the perceiver's own proximity or distance to a target of stereotype and this particular identity). One of many categories would be thus a focal category. For example, a woman would always foreground another woman's identity as a woman, ignoring or deprioritising her other identities. Accordingly, she would stereotype the other woman with gendered/female content rather than racial content. Thirdly, social context may inform which intersecting identities of the target are emphasised by a perceiver, or even recognised. It could be the intersection of gender and race in one, and of race and age, in another social context (Petsko and Bodenhausen 2020).

Similarly, Hall et al. (2019) propose in their model of stereotyping that categories may be implicitly connected (associated): either on the basis of their phenotypic similarity or stereotypical overlap. In the model of phenotypical similarity, a perceiver can link two or more categories to shared appearance attributes. Race and class, race and gender, and ethnicity and religion seem to be such associated categories (Hall et al. 2019). Researchers could demonstrate that Sikhs are 'mistaken' for Muslims because of their phenotypical similarity to people who are Muslims. As such 'mistakes' became more common in the aftermath of 9/11 (Jhutti-Johal and Singh 2020), a geographical (Pauker et al. 2018) and historical context seems to play a role here as well. In the stereotypical overlap, two or more categories 'share' a stereotype, which leads for example to misperceptions of black and Asian faces (Stolier and Freeman 2016; Ahluwalia and Pellettiere 2010). Johnson et al. (2012) suggest that a racial phenotype, for example 'Asian', shares features with a female phenotype, and a 'Black' phenotype with a male phenotype. In turn, Asian women would be recognised faster as women than Asian men as men, and so on. Yet, so far, this research could not establish the direction of causality of this process, that is, whether 'facial characteristics' or stereotyped attributes shape intersectional perception (Kim et al. 2015).[10]

If some categories or their intersections are foregrounded in a certain social context, as suggested by Petsko and Bodenhausen (2020), the question is, what causes perceivers to attend to some identities and not to others? Petsko and Bodenhausen (2020) suggest four possible reasons for foregrounding: category accessibility, perceiver goals, category fit, and category distinctiveness. A category which is more easily retrieved from memory (is more accessible) may be preferred (foregrounded) despite the intersectionality of the target. For example, perceivers with high levels of racial prejudice are more likely to use race and not gender to stereotype a person. Or perceivers may accentuate this category which is better aligned with their goals than another category. Someone 'focused' on women for some reason would rather 'see' women among people of different skin pigmentation, than men. A third possibility is that a category itself may fit the social context better than another one, in normative or comparative terms. Finally, more distinctive categories could be more attention-grabbing: among all white men, a white woman would be more likely to be perceived as a woman (gender differentiates her from the group), in comparison to a situation when a non-white woman is surrounded by other white women (here her gender is not a distinctive category). Finally, it seems that people tend to categorise others slower if requested to 'order' the targets to intersectional (e.g., Asian woman) rather than to a single (e.g., Asian, or woman) category (Remedios and Snyder 2018). All of the models of intersectional stereotyping considered so far suggest that attention, salience, and exposure matter for how people are perceived.

Attention: Exposure, Salience, Foregrounding

Attention is necessarily selective. The process of focusing attention on something or someone implies exclusion; inattentiveness is thus an effect of being attentive. It means also that something or someone is visible in effect to the extent to which the viewer attends to, or, in other words, that visibility is a function of attention (Zerubavel 2015: 2). We are not necessarily conscious about what we attend to and what we ignore, but attention can be socially trained. Attention is thus a socio-mental act. Zerubavel (2015) claims that attention and inattention are conventionally delineated. Thus, people are members of attentional cultures and subcultures: I might be 'trained' in my socialisation as a girl and woman to pay attention to children as this is demanded from women in my culture, and I might be 'trained' to pay attention to signs of sexism as a scholar within a university subculture.

What is worth, or what necessitates, one's attention is normative, for it is subject to a social norm, and it could be a moral imperative; as a mother I often experience moral judgements on whether I sufficiently pay attention to my child climbing a boulder wall at the playground, at least when the child is young. Me paying attention to my teenage son at a boulder wall would be less accepted or even morally rejected as exaggerated care. My gazing at a bouldering man could be interpreted as sexualised interest in this person if I ignore other boulderers, and so on.

Similarly, inattention is learnt in a social context.[11] Ignoring others to some degree has been described as a modern urban phenomenon, for example by the sociologist Erwin Goffman. Studying the everyday life in a city, Goffman called one pattern of people's behaviour 'civil inattention', a display of disinterestedness which does not signal disregard of the other person. In this sense, inattention is more than just the lack of a gaze; it is a certain kind of social relation and a competence to refuse relations without creating non-persons (Goffman 1963). Such competence is important to establish conviviality in settings which do not allow for much physical distance but require social detachment, such as a public elevator cabin, studied ethnographically by Stefan Hirschauer (2005), a crowded metro platform, a train, and so on. Inattention, in the sense of being attentive only for a short while—or the capacity to redirect attention quickly—is a principle of modern capitalism which profits from us shifting attention from one object to another, from one product to another, and seeking not just a new object, but something new, surprising, outstanding, and extraordinary—attention-catching (Schroer 2019). Producing (visual) attentiveness thus is considered a feature of modern industries.

At the same time, there are areas in which inattention is undesired, even dangerous, and sanctioned. Crary (1999) shows that the modern highly specialised industrial production requires workers to be focused and attentive to just one particular aspect of the process. Attention, and sanctioning of distraction, goes hand in hand with increasing specialisation of professions, including scientific enquiry. A modern subject—an individual—is self-disciplined, focused, attentive (Reckwitz 2004). If it fails to bring attention, it is to be blamed for its own failures. Attentiveness is thus a (western) modern technological and economic imperative. Inattention can also be pathologised: we can think of the attention deficit disorder (ADD) diagnosed frequently in children that causes a range of behavioural patterns such as difficulty attending to instruction, focusing on schoolwork, keeping up with assignments, or completing complex tasks.

Attention is thus more than a gaze or looking. First, focusing attention is multimodal; it encompasses vision as much as other senses. By attending to something or someone, this mixed modality becomes irreducible (Crary 1999: 3). Second, attention should be conceived of as a model of subjectivity that emerged in western modernity (Crary 1999; see also Schroer 2019; Wehrle 2013). It was made possible by various social and technological developments—in this sense, as Crary (1999) argues, attention is an effect of different forces and relations of power in modernity and not simply a domain of the visual. An attentive subject, and a subject of attention, in (western) modernity is a subject whose capacity to perceive is located within the body; in turn, the attentive subject is isolated from other people and separated from the environment (Crary 1999: 3). Disintegration of an attentive subject and the surroundings opens up the space for technical and psychological manipulations of (visual) perception (through various technologies of attraction or scientific experiments in psychological research on stereotyping). Crary (1999: 25) argues that the centring of the concept of attention in (western) modernity results in a larger set of positions and consequences for thinking of related issues; for example, understanding of attraction as a competence which can be trained and manipulated results in the idea of human perception as 'impure': any sensation can thus be understood as compounding of memory, desire, will, anticipation and immediate experience. In this sense, perception—or specifically seeing—cannot be reduced to visuality. The difference that we 'see' is not the one located in the body of the other, nor is it embodied by the observer, but happens in-between the body of the other and the perceiver, an effect of relations of power. Alternative vision is constituted in modernity as another cognitive bodily state (trance, reverie, hallucination). In turn, the centrality of attention in (western) modernity disempowers the subject, stripping it of the power to act and the power to resist (Crary 1999: 3).

Through the lens of attention, the main question is how our perception of others as members of one, or more, or all or no categories is fashioned by powers external to the perceiver and to the target. It exceeds the scope of this chapter to discuss in detail all proposals for how societal values and norms are incorporated by individuals and transformed into their personal convictions. Generally, scholars in various disciplines (philosophy, sociology, anthropology, linguistics, political science, psychology, and cognitive science) use the terms 'scheme' and 'frame' referring to internal mental structures and external, 'cultural', patterns (Lizardo 2016b; Wood et al. 2018). One possibility to conceptualise the relation between public 'culture' and individual perception is to consider how social frames evoke meanings and activate schemes. The last could be understood as embodied multi-modal experience, stored in memory, nondeclarative and habituative, flexible patterns of interpretation which do not have any specific content, and can thus be transposable across variable situations (Wood et al. 2018). Importantly, such personal schemes can be altered through repeated experience, yet this process is slow (Lizardo 2016a), as suggested by the research on the 'predictive brain' (Hinton 2017).

My own research suggests that some situations (frames, in the terminology of Wood et al. 2018) may speed up the re-learning process, or at least disrupt personal schemes to some extent. Researching Polish migrants in Germany, we noticed that they constantly refer to other people's ethnicity in narrating about their daily life and surroundings (Lisiak and Nowicka 2018). Ethnicity appears to be a basic operator, a practical category with which they perceive other's difference (Brubaker et al. 2004), in particular when others' difference is juxtaposed with their own identity as Polish. Yet their narrations also include many references to irritating situations or the feeling of a certain discomfort, or even annoyance. These narrations assigned positive or negative judgements to people's behaviour or utterance using ethnic labels, yet the irritations were caused by a perceived mismatch or uneasiness between their own practices in a new context. Polish migrants frequently identified—but could rarely express it explicitly—a different pace of doing things in Poland and in Germany, and more generally, people's different approach to time. This manifests in the speed at which people try to complete certain tasks, if they work over hours, how they spend their leisure time, or if they make investments in their own or their children's future career by attending additional courses, and so on. Such approaches to time (personal schemes) respond to neoliberal imperatives of 'good worker', or 'good mother' that are embedded local contexts (frames) in Poland or Germany. By migrating between these contexts, people we interviewed experience a sense of the misalignment of their own practice to that of their surroundings. They become attentive to what otherwise remained hidden to them.

Stoltz and Taylor (2017) remind us that material context matters for attentiveness. Placing objects in an unusual way or location makes them more perceptible, exposed, and foregrounded. We could think of a luxurious car parked in a poor neighbourhood, or a black female parliament member in a parliamentary assembly room occupied by white male members. Discussing attention requires thus to consider materiality and the meaning given to the target of perception. Any purposeful enunciation or manipulation of attention relies on these two aspects: we can think of subversion, controversy, or resistance in artistic practice achieved by placing objects outside of their usual context to evoke irritation or surprise, reverse conventional attentional patters, re-direct the attention to what we habitually background, and lend the object or situation a new meaning (Zerubavel 2015: 8).

Conclusions

We learn from cognitive science that categories—understood as a mode of (visual) experience of the world—are an effective way of making judgements and taking decisions. With categories, humans reduce the complex sensory (visual) input and create mental representations of the world

(Gärdenfors 2019). In this sense, categories are 'useful' to navigate the world, but also necessarily 'flawed'. Or, they 'hinder' us from seeing the world 'as it is'. Contemporary cognitive scientists no longer presume that categories are determined by physical (i.e., located 'in the world') or physiological (i.e., located 'in the brain') principles (Jraissati 2019: 422). The consensus on the lack of such nativist determinism does not mean that categories can easily be changed. Our perception is structured, and culture (including language) plays a role in how it is structured. It is a subject of intense efforts in cognitive science to understand how we decide on assigning an object to a particular category. The culturally shaped and shared concepts may 'help us' in this cognitive decision (Deroy 2019).

Categories create a horizon of our experience in the world, yet the experience (seeing) of the world and representation of it do not match perfectly. In this 'gap', there is room for change, even if we tend to rely on the supposed visual evidentiality of difference and similarity. We are attentive to some aspects and ignore others; in the culture which assigns meaning both to visual experience and to the concepts of race and gender, the principle of categorisation and the factors in social stratification mix, and social inequalities become stabilised with recourse to the supposed visual evidence. But if confronted with the unexpected, we can revise and 'recalibrate' our predictions and perceptions. This is where we imagine the potential for artistic interventions. Art can encourage new ways of 'seeing' and shift the boundaries which we apply on otherwise continuous nature of visually accessible objects, including bodies, their shapes and skin tones.

The challenge of the scientific gaze remains. Sciences use categories in multiple and often unreflexive ways and contribute to their fixation. For example, mono-categories are routinely used in experimental psychology to examine stereotyping. Complex concepts such as race are at times reduced to simple categories (resulting in colourism). Categories often are used in simplified additive way, for example in social surveys in sociology, health, or education studies (Bauer et al. 2021). Categories in the sciences are used to denote a mode of perception (to 'order the world'), a mode of experience, and/or as an analytical lens to explain human perception and/or experience of difference. References to visual, sensory experience and the visually accessible features of objects crosscut each of these usages, contributing to the confusion rather than resolving it.

The challenge is not the lack of exchange between critical theory and cognitive science—we can think of the cognitive turn in sociology starting with Habermas, the attempts to integrate the socio-cultural and naturalistic approaches in cognitive sociology, or the influence of critical theory in psychology leading to the development of critical psychology (cf. Teo 2014; Strydom 2019)—but rather the routine application of categories of race or gender in empirical and experimental studies. In this sense, there is perhaps sufficient mutual influence between critical theory and the sciences on the level of theory, but insufficient transformation regarding the methodologies. It requires thus a change of scientific culture to enable more intersectional seeing.

Notes

1. Cognitive science is an interdisciplinary field of studies on the mind and its processes. Cognitive scientists borrow from linguistics, psychology, Artificial Intelligence, philosophy, neuroscience, and anthropology to understand phenomena such as remembering, visual perception, or the acquisition of language.
2. All names of interview partners are fictitious.
3. The quote is taken from an interview conducted by the TRANSFORmIG project (ERC Grant No 313369 awarded to Magdalena Nowicka, 2013–2018) team. More information on the project, its design, and the sample can be found in various articles published by Nowicka. The quotation and its analysis were published in Wojnicka and Nowicka (2021). The analysis of the interviews uses the wording of the research participants even though some expressions might not be common any longer in scientific discourse and beyond it in the Anglophone world. The interviewed migrants self-identified as Polish.
4. Interviewed by Agata Lisiak in the course of the TRANSFORmIG project (Lisiak 2017).
5. All 2011 interviews were conducted in the course of the project by Magdalena Nowicka and financed by the Max-Planck Institute for the Study of Religious and Ethnic Diversity (research fellowship 2010–2013).
6. He mistakes ciabatta, an Italian bread made of white flower, with chapati Indian flat bread.
7. This and the following quotation come from two interviews conducted in 2014 within the TRANSFORmIG Project.
8. The US Census from 2013 finds that 6.9% Americans, that is about nine million chose two or more racial categories when asked about their race. One-in-seven US infants (14%) were multiracial or multiethnic in 2015, nearly triple the share than in 1980, according to a Pew Research Center analysis of Census Bureau data. Mixed-race people are the fastest growing

ethnic group in the UK. In the last 2011 census, 1.25 million respondents, which is double as many as in the 2001 census, self-identified as mixed-race.
9. This body of research routinely refers to race or racial groups, which stands at odds with the scientific consensus that there are no biological races. Assuming that the authors use race or racial group to designate categories of social identity, all references to race are put here in quotation marks to stress the social character of these concepts.
10. Experimental studies on cognition and stereotyping often use software to modify gender and racial facial characteristics. It is unclear whether the software, like face recognition software, is already racially biased, which could in turn impact the research results. Possibly, the modifications correspond to a spectrum of face characteristics, but the categorisation done for the purpose of data analysis could be biased.
11. Inattention is also learnt by Artificial Intelligence software which can lead to racial bias (cf. Bacchini and Lorusso 2019).

WORKS CITED

Adamczak-Krysztofowicz, Sylwia, and Anna Szczepaniak-Kozak. 2017. A Disturbing View of Intercultural Communication: Findings of a Study into Hate Speech in Polish. *Linguistica Silesiana* 38: 285–310.

Ahluwalia, Muninder K., and Laura Pellettiere. 2010. Sikh Men Post-9/11: Misidentification, Discrimination, and Coping. *Asian American Journal of Psychology* 1 (4): 303–314. https://doi.org/10.1037/a0022156.

Ahmed, Sara. 2007. A Phenomenology of Whiteness. *Feminist Theory* 8 (2): 149–168. https://doi.org/10.1177/1464700107078139.

Ainsworth, Claire. 2015. Sex Redefined. *Nature* 518 (7539): 288–291. https://doi.org/10.1038/518288a.

Ali, Suki. 2003. *Mixed-Race, Post-Race: Gender, New Ethnicities, and Cultural Practices*. Oxford: Berg.

Anthias, Floya. 2008. Thinking through the Lens of Translocational Positionality: An Intersectionality Frame for Understanding Identity and Belonging. *Translocations: Migration and Social Change* 4 (1): 5–20.

Anzures, Gizelle, Paul C. Quinn, Olivier Pascalis, Alan M. Slater, and Kang Lee. 2010. Categorization, Categorical Perception, and Asymmetry in Infants' Representation of Face Race. *Developmental Science* 13 (4): 553–564. https://doi.org/10.1111/j.1467-7687.2009.00900.x.

Aspinall, Peter J., and Miri Song. 2014. *Mixed Race Identities*. London: Palgrave Macmillan.

Ásta. 2018. *Categories We Live by: The Construction of Sex, Gender, Race, and Other Social Categories*. New York: Oxford University Press.

Avargues-Weber, Aurore, and Martin Giurfa. 2015. Conceptual Learning by Miniature Brains. In *The Conceptual Mind: New Directions in the Study of Concepts*, eds. Eric Margolis, and Stephen Laurence, 3–28. Cambridge: MIT Press.

Bacchini, Fabio, and Ludovica Lorusso. 2019. Race, Again: How Face Recognition Technology Reinforces Racial Discrimination. *JICES* 17 (3): 321–335. https://doi.org/10.1108/JICES-05-2018-0050.

Bastian, Brock, and Nick Haslam. 2007. Psychological Essentialism and Attention Allocation: Preferences for Stereotype-Consistent versus Stereotype-Inconsistent Information. *The Journal of Social Psychology* 147 (5): 531–541. https://doi.org/10.3200/SOCP.147.5.531-542.

Bauer, Greta R., Siobhan M. Churchill, Mayuri Mahendran, Chantel Walwyn, Daniel Lizotte, and Alma Angelica Villa-Rueda. 2021. Intersectionality in Quantitative Research: A Systematic Review of Its Emergence and Applications of Theory and Methods. *SSM—Population Health* 14. https://doi.org/10.1016/j.ssmph.2021.100798.

Beaudevin, Claire, and Katharina Schramm. 2019. Sorting, Typing, Classifying. *MAT* 6 (4). https://doi.org/10.17157/mat.6.4.767.

Bech, Henning. 2014. Missing from Masculinity Studies: Aesthetics, Ethics, Existence. *Masculinities: A Journal of Identity and Culture* 1 (2): 6–30.

Bigler, Rebecca S., and Lynn S. Liben. 2006. A Developmental Intergroup Theory of Social Stereotypes and Prejudice. *Advances in Child Development and Behavior 34*: 39–89.

Boatright-Horowitz, Su L., Marisa E. Marraccini, and Yvette Harps-Logan. 2012. Teaching Antiracism: College Students' Emotional and Cognitive Reactions to Learning About White Privilege. *Journal of Black Studies* 43 (8): 893–911.

Bonnett, Alastair. 1998. Who Was White? The Disappearance of Non-European White Identities and the Formation of European Racial Whiteness. *Ethnic and Racial Studies* 21 (6): 1029–1055.

Bordalo, Pedro, Katherine Coffman, Nicola Gennaioli, and Andrei Shleifer. 2016. Stereotypes*. *The Quarterly Journal of Economics* 131 (4): 1753–1794. https://doi.org/10.1093/qje/qjw029.

Böröcz, József, and Mahua Sarkar. 2017. The Unbearable Whiteness of the Polish Plumber and the Hungarian Peacock Dance Around "Race". *Slavic Review* 76 (2): 307–314.

Bourdieu, Pierre. 1977. *Outline of a Theory of Practice*. Cambridge: Cambridge University Press.

———. 1984. *Distinction: A Social Critique of the Judgement of Taste*. Cambridge: Harvard University Press.

Brighenti, Andrea Mubi. 2010. *Visibility in Social Theory and Social Research*. Basingstoke: Palgrave Macmillan.

Brooks, Jeffrey A., Ryan M. Stolier, and Jonathan B. Freeman. 2018. Stereotypes Bias Visual Prototypes for Sex and Emotion Categories. *Social Cognition* 36 (5): 481–493. https://doi.org/10.1521/soco.2018.36.5.481.

Brubaker, Rogers, Mara Loveman, and Peter Stamatov. 2004. Ethnicity as Cognition. *Theory and Society* 33 (1): 31–64. https://doi.org/10.1023/B:RYSO.0000021405.18890.63.

Campion, Karis. 2019. "You Think You're Black?" Exploring Black Mixed-Race Experiences of Black Rejection. *Ethnic and Racial Studies* 42 (16): 196–213. https://doi.org/10.1080/01419870.2019.1642503.

Cassese, Erin C. 2019. Intersectional Stereotyping in Political Decision Making. In *Oxford Research Encyclopedia of Politics*. https://oxfordre.com/politics/view/10.1093/acrefore/9780190228637.001.0001/acrefore-9780190228637-e-773.

Chaney, Kimberly E., Diana T. Sanchez, and Lina Saud. 2020. White Categorical Ambiguity: Exclusion of Middle Eastern Americans from the White Racial Category. *Social Psychological and Personality Science* 194855062093054. https://doi.org/10.1177/1948550620930546.

Chen, Jacqueline M., and David L. Hamilton. 2012. Natural Ambiguities: Racial Categorization of Multiracial Individuals. *Journal of Experimental Social Psychology* 48 (1): 152–164. https://doi.org/10.1016/j.jesp.2011.10.005.

Cichy, Radoslaw M., Dimitrios Pantazis, and Aude Oliva. 2014. Resolving Human Object Recognition in Space and Time. *Nature Neuroscience* 17 (3): 455–462. https://doi.org/10.1038/nn.3635.

Clark, Andy. 2013. Whatever Next? Predictive Brains, Situated Agents, and the Future of Cognitive Science. *Behavioral and Brain Sciences* 36 (3): 181–204. https://doi.org/10.1017/S0140525X12000477.

———. 2014. Perceiving as Predicting. In *Perception and Its Modalities*, eds. Andy Clark, Dustin Stokes, Mohan Matthen, and Stephen Biggs, 23–43. New York: Oxford University Press.

Cohen, Henri, and Claire Lefebvre, eds. 2017. *Handbook of Categorization in Cognitive Science*. 2nd edition. Saint Louis: Elsevier Science.

Collins, Patricia Hill. 2019. *Intersectionality: As Critical Social Theory*. Durham: Duke University Press.

Costandi, Mo. 2012. Racial Bias Colours Visual Perception. *Nature*. https://doi.org/10.1038/nature.2012.10961.

Cowan, Nelson. 2015. George Miller's Magical Number of Immediate Memory in Retrospect: Observations on the Faltering Progression of Science. *Psychological Review* 122 (3): 536–541. https://doi.org/10.1037/a0039035.

Crane, Tim, and Craig French. 2017. The Problem of Perception. In *The Stanford Encyclopedia of Philosophy (Spring 2017 Edition)*, ed. Edward N. Zalta. https://plato.stanford.edu/archives/spr2017/entries/perception-problem.

Crary, Jonathan. 1999. *Suspensions of Perception: Attention, Spectacle, and Modern Culture*. Cambridge: MIT Press.
Deroy, Ophelia. 2013. Object-Sensitivity Versus Cognitive Penetrability of Perception. *Philos Stud* 162 (1): 87–107. https://doi.org/10.1007/s11098-012-9989-1.
———. 2019. Categorising Without Concepts. *Review of Philosophy and Psychology* 10 (3): 465–478. https://doi.org/10.1007/s13164-019-00431-2.
Devine, Patricia G., and Steven J. Sherman. 1992. Intuitive Versus Rational Judgment and the Role of Stereotyping in the Human Condition: Kirk or Spock? *Psychological Inquiry* 3 (2): 153–159.
Doorley, Karina, and Eva Sierminska. 2015. Myth or Fact? The Beauty Premium Across the Wage Distribution in Germany. *Economics Letters* 129: 29–34. https://doi.org/10.1016/j.econlet.2015.01.033.
Fanon, Frantz. 1986. *Black Skin, White Masks*. London: Pluto.
Feliciano, Cynthia. 2015. Shades of Race. *American Behavioral Scientist* 60 (4): 390–419. https://doi.org/10.1177/0002764215613401.
Fiałkowska, Kamila. 2018. Cyber Space: A Refuge for Hegemonic Masculinity Among Polish Migrants in the UK. In *Gender and Migration. A Gender-Sensitive Approach to Migration Dynamics*, eds. Christiane Timmerman, Maria Lucinda Fonseca, Lore Van Praag, and Sonia Pereira, 95–118. Leuven: Leuven University Press.
Firestone, Chaz, and Brian J. Scholl. 2016. Seeing and Thinking: Foundational Issues and Empirical Horizons. *The Behavioral and Brain Sciences* 39: e264. https://doi.org/10.1017/S0140525X16000029.
Folstein, Jonathan, Thomas J. Palmeri, Ana E. van Gulick, and Isabel Gauthier. 2015. Category Learning Stretches Neural Representations in Visual Cortex. *Current Directions in Psychological Science* 24 (1): 17–23. https://doi.org/10.1177/0963721414550707.
Fox, Jon E., and Magda Mogilnicka. 2019. Pathological Integration, Or, How East Europeans Use Racism to Become British. *The British Journal of Sociology* 70 (1): 5–23. https://doi.org/10.1111/1468-4446.12337.
Fox, Jon E., Laura Moroşanu, and Eszter Szilassy. 2012. The Racialization of the New European Migration to the UK. *Sociology* 46 (4): 680–695.
———. 2015. Denying Discrimination: Status, 'Race', and the Whitening of Britain's New Europeans. *Journal of Ethnic and Migration Studies* 41 (5): 729–748. https://doi.org/10.1080/1369183X.2014.962491.
Fox, Robin. 1992. Prejudice and the Unfinished Mind: A New Look at an Old Failing. *Psychological Inquiry* 3 (2): 137–152.
Franklin, Anna. 2016. Infant Color Categories. In *Encyclopedia of Color Science and Technology*. Vol. 13, ed. Ronnier Luo, 1–7. Berlin/Heidelberg: Springer.
Freeman, Jonathan B., Yina Ma, Shihui Han, and Nalini Ambady. 2013. Influences of Culture and Visual Context on Real-Time Social Categorization. *Journal of*

Experimental Social Psychology 49 (2): 206–210. https://doi.org/10.1016/j.jesp.2012.10.015.

Freeman, Jonathan B., Kristin Pauker, and Diana T. Sanchez. 2016. A Perceptual Pathway to Bias: Interracial Exposure Reduces Abrupt Shifts in Real-Time Race Perception That Predict Mixed-Race Bias. *Psychological Science* 27 (4): 502–517. https://doi.org/10.1177/0956797615627418.

Gärdenfors, Peter. 2019. From Sensations to Concepts: A Proposal for Two Learning Processes. *Review of Philosophy and Psychology* 10 (3): 441–464. https://doi.org/10.1007/s13164-017-0379-7.

Gawlewicz, Anna. 2015. Production and Transnational Transfer of the Language of Difference: The Effects of Polish Migrants' Encounters with Superdiversity. *Central and Eastern European Migration Review* 4: 25–42.

Gelman, Susan A. 2003. *The Essential Child: Origins of Essentialism in Everyday Thought*. Oxford: Oxford University Press.

Ghavami, Negin, and Letitia A. Peplau. 2013. An Intersectional Analysis of Gender and Ethnic Stereotypes. *Psychology of Women Quarterly* 37 (1): 113–127. https://doi.org/10.1177/0361684312464203.

Gibson, James J. 1979. *The Ecological Approach to Visual Perception*. Boston: Houghton Mifflin.

Goffman, Erving. 1963. *Behavior in Public Places: Notes on the Social Organization of Gatherings*. London: Free Press.

Grier, Tiffanie, Carol Rambo, and Marshall A. Taylor. 2014. "What Are You?": Racial Ambiguity, Stigma, and the Racial Formation Project. *Deviant Behavior* 35 (12): 1006–1022. https://doi.org/10.1080/01639625.2014.901081.

Grosz, Elizabeth. 1993. "Bodies and Knowledges: Feminism and the Crisis of Reason." In *Feminist Epistemologies*, eds. Linda Alcoff, and Elizabeth Potter, 187–216. New York: Routledge.

Halford, Graeme S., and Trevor J. Hine. 2016. Fundamental Differences between Perception and Cognition aside from Cognitive Penetrability. *The Behavioral and Brain Sciences* 39:e247. https://doi.org/10.1017/S0140525X15002526.

Hall, Erika V., Alison V. Hall, Adam D. Galinsky, and Katherine W. Phillips. 2019. MOSAIC: A Model of Stereotyping Through Associated and Intersectional Categories. *AMR* 44 (3): 643–672. https://doi.org/10.5465/amr.2017.0109.

Hall, Stuart. 2017. *Familiar Stranger: A Life Between Two Islands*. Durham: Duke University Press.

Hampton, James A. 1998. Similarity-Based Categorization and Fuzziness of Natural Categories. *Cognition* 65 (2): 137–165. https://doi.org/10.1016/S0010-0277(97)00042-5.

Harnad, Steven. 2017. To Cognize Is to Categorize: Cognition Is Categorization. In *Handbook of Categorization in Cognitive Science*, eds. Henri Cohen, and Claire Lefebvre, 23–53. 2nd edition. Saint Louis: Elsevier Science.

Harrits, Gitte S., and Helene H. Pedersen. 2018. Class Categories and the Subjective Dimension of Class: The Case of Denmark. *The British Journal of Sociology* 69 (1): 67–98. https://doi.org/10.1111/1468-4446.12282.

Herman, Melissa R. 2010. Do You See What I Am? *Social Psychology Quarterly* 73 (1): 58–78. https://doi.org/10.1177/0190272510361436.

Hernando, Almudena. 2017. *The Fantasy of Individuality: On the Sociohistorical Construction of the Modern Subject*. Cham: Springer.

Hinton, Perry. 2017. Implicit Stereotypes and the Predictive Brain: Cognition and Culture in "Biased" Person Perception. *Palgrave Communications* 3 (1): 1–9. https://doi.org/10.1057/palcomms.2017.86.

Hirschauer, Stefan. 2005. On Doing Being a Stranger: The Practical Constitution of Civil Inattention. *Journal for the Theory of Social Behaviour* 35 (1): 41–67. https://doi.org/10.1111/j.0021-8308.2005.00263.x.

Hirschfeld, Lawrence. 1996. *Race in the Making: Cognition, Culture, and the Child's Construction of Human Kinds*. Cambridge: MIT Press.

Hoyt, Crystal L., Thekla Morgenroth, and Jeni L. Burnette. 2019. Understanding Sexual Prejudice: The Role of Political Ideology and Strategic Essentialism. *Journal of Applied Social Psychology* 49 (1): 3–14. https://doi.org/10.1111/jasp.12560.

Hunt, Linda M., and Mary S. Megyesi. 2008. The Ambiguous Meanings of the Racial/Ethnic Categories Routinely Used in Human Genetics Research. *Social Science & Medicine (1982)* 66 (2): 349–361. https://doi.org/10.1016/j.socscimed.2007.08.034.

Ignatiev, Noel. 1995. *How the Irish Became White*. New York: Routledge.

Ingold, Tim. 2018. Back to the Future with the Theory of Affordances. *HAU: Journal of Ethnographic Theory* 8 (1–2): 39–44. https://doi.org/10.1086/698358.

Ito, Tiffany A., and Silvia Tomelleri. 2017. Seeing Is Not Stereotyping: The Functional Independence of Categorization and Stereotype Activation. *Social Cognitive and Affective Neuroscience* 12 (5): 758–764. https://doi.org/10.1093/scan/nsx009.

Jhutti-Johal, Jagbir, and Hardeep Singh. 2020. *Racialization, Islamophobia and Mistaken Identity: The Sikh Experience*. Abingdon/New York: Routledge.

Johnson, Kerri L., Jonathan B. Freeman, and Kristin Pauker. 2012. Race Is Gendered: How Covarying Phenotypes and Stereotypes Bias Sex Categorization. *Journal of Personality and Social Psychology* 102 (1): 116–131. https://doi.org/10.1037/a0025335.

Johnston, Linda. 2005. Man: Woman. In *Spaces of Geographical Thought: Deconstructing Human Geography's Binaries*, eds. Paul Cloke, and Ron Johnston, 119–141. London: SAGE.

Jraissati, Yasmina. 2019. Editorial: Sensory Categories. *Review of Philosophy and Psychology* 10 (3): 419–439. https://doi.org/10.1007/s13164-019-00439-8.

Kahneman, Daniel, and Amos Tversky. 1972. Subjective Probability: A Judgment of Representativeness. *Cognitive Psychology* 3 (3): 430–454. https://doi.org/10.1016/0010-0285(72)90016-3.

———. 1973. On the Psychology of Prediction. *Psychological Review* 80 (4): 237–251. https://doi.org/10.1037/H0034747.

Kalev, Alexandra, Frank Dobbin, and Erin Kelly. 2006. Best Practices or Best Guesses? Assessing the Efficacy of Corporate Affirmative Action and Diversity Policies. *American Sociological Review* 71 (4): 589–617. https://doi.org/10.1177/000312240607100404.

Kang, Sonia K., and Alison L. Chasteen. 2009. Beyond the Double-Jeopardy Hypothesis: Assessing Emotion on the Faces of Multiply-Categorizable Targets of Prejudice. *Journal of Experimental Social Psychology* 45 (6): 1281–1285. https://doi.org/10.1016/j.jesp.2009.07.002.

Khanna, Nikki. 2010. "If You're Half Black, You're Just Black": Reflected Appraisals and the Persistence of the One-Drop Rule. *The Sociological Quarterly* 51 (1): 96–121. https://doi.org/10.1111/j.1533-8525.2009.01162.x.

Kim, Hojin I., Kerri L. Johnson, and Scott P. Johnson. 2015. Gendered Race: Are Infants' Face Preferences Guided by Intersectionality of Sex and Race? *Frontiers in Psychology* 6: 1330. https://doi.org/10.3389/fpsyg.2015.01330.

Kousta, Stavroula-Thaleia, Gabriella Vigliocco, David P. Vinson, Mark Andrews, and Elena Del Campo. 2011. The Representation of Abstract Words: Why Emotion Matters. *Journal of Experimental Psychology. General* 140 (1): 14–34. https://doi.org/10.1037/a0021446.

Kraus, Michael W., and Jacinth J.X. Tan. 2015. Americans Overestimate Social Class Mobility. *Journal of Experimental Social Psychology* 58 (6): 101–111. https://doi.org/10.1016/j.jesp.2015.01.005.

Kress, Gunther, and Theo van Leeuwen. 1996. *Reading Images: The Grammar of Visual Design*. London: Routledge.

Lai, Calvin K., Allison L. Skinner, Erin Cooley, Sohad Murrar, Markus Brauer, Thierry Devos, Jimmy Calanchini et al. 2016. Reducing Implicit Racial Preferences: II. Intervention Effectiveness Across Time. *Journal of Experimental Psychology. General* 145 (8): 1001–1016. https://doi.org/10.1037/xge0000179.

Lakoff, George. 2014. Mapping the Brain's Metaphor Circuitry: Metaphorical Thought in Everyday Reason. *Frontiers in Human Neuroscience* 8: 958. https://doi.org/10.3389/fnhum.2014.00958.

Lamer, Sarah A., Timothy D. Sweeny, Michael L. Dyer, and Max Weisbuch. 2018. Rapid Visual Perception of Interracial Crowds: Racial Category Learning from Emotional Segregation. *Journal of Experimental Psychology. General* 147 (5): 683–701. https://doi.org/10.1037/xge0000443.

Lapiņa, Linda, and Mantė Vertelytė. 2020. "Eastern European", Yes, but How? Autoethnographic Accounts of Differentiated Whiteness. *NORA—Nordic*

Journal of Feminist and Gender Research 28 (3): 237–250. https://doi.org/10.1080/08038740.2020.1762731.

Leckcivilize, Attakrit, and Alexander Straub. 2018. Headscarf and Job Recruitment—Lifting the Veil of Labour Market Discrimination. *IZA Journal of Labor Economics* 7 (1): 521. https://doi.org/10.1186/s40172-018-0071-x.

Lee, Kang, Paul C. Quinn, and Olivier Pascalis. 2017. Face Race Processing and Racial Bias in Early Development: A Perceptual-Social Linkage. *Current Directions in Psychological Science* 26 (3): 256–262. https://doi.org/10.1177/0963721417690276.

Levin, Daniel T. 2000. Race as a Visual Feature: Using Visual Search and Perceptual Discrimination Tasks to Understand Face Categories and the Cross-Race Recognition Deficit. *Journal of Experimental Psychology: General* 129 (4): 559–574. https://doi.org/10.1037/0096-3445.129.4.559.

Lisiak, Agata. 2017. Other Mothers: Encountering In/Visible Femininities in Migration and Urban Contexts. *Feminist Review* 117 (1): 41–55. https://doi.org/10.1057/s41305-017-0086-3.

Lisiak, Agata, and Magdalena Nowicka. 2018. Tacit Differences, Ethnicity and Neoliberalism: Polish Migrant Mothers in German Cities. *Gender, Place & Culture* 25 (6): 899–915. https://doi.org/10.1080/0966369X.2017.1334631.

Lizardo, Omar. 2016a. Cultural Symbols and Cultural Power. *Qualitative Sociology* 39 (2): 199–204. https://doi.org/10.1007/s11133-016-9329-4.

———. 2016b. Improving Cultural Analysis. *American Sociological Review* 82 (1): 88–115. https://doi.org/10.1177/0003122416675175.

Lovén, Johanna, Jenny Rehnman, Stefan Wiens, Torun Lindholm, Nathalie Peira, and Agneta Herlitz. 2012. Who Are You Looking at? The Influence of Face Gender on Visual Attention and Memory for Own- and Other-Race Faces. *Memory (Hove, England)* 20 (4): 321–331. https://doi.org/10.1080/09658211.2012.658064.

Ludwig, Rita M., and Michael W. Kraus. 2019. *Neighborhood Characteristics and Individual Perception of Social Inequity—a Stage 1 Registered Report*.

MacLin, Otto H., and Roy S. Malpass. 2001. Racial Categorization of Faces: The Ambiguous Race Face Effect. *Psychology, Public Policy, and Law* 7 (1): 98–118. https://doi.org/10.1037/1076-8971.7.1.98.

Medin, Douglas, and Andrew Ortony. 1989. Comments on Part I: Psychological Essentialism. In *Similarity and Analogical Reasoning*, eds. Andrew Ortony, and Stella Vosniadou, 179–196. Cambridge: Cambridge University Press.

Meissner, Christian A., and John C. Brigham. 2001. Thirty Years of Investigating the Own-Race Bias in Memory for Faces: A Meta-Analytic Review. *Psychology, Public Policy, and Law* 7 (1): 3–35. https://doi.org/10.1037/1076-8971.7.1.3.

Mol, A., and J. Law. 1994. Regions, Networks and Fluids: Anaemia and Social Topology. *Social Studies of Science* 24 (4): 641–671. https://doi.org/10.1177/030631279402400402.

Montemayor, Carlos, and Harry H. Haladjian. 2017. Perception and Cognition Are Largely Independent, but Still Affect Each Other in Systematic Ways: Arguments from Evolution and the Consciousness-Attention Dissociation. *Frontiers in Psychology* 8: 40. https://doi.org/10.3389/fpsyg.2017.00040.

Narayan, Uma. 1997. *Dislocating Cultures: Identities, Traditions, and Third-World Feminism.* New York: Routledge.

Nietzsche, Friedrich. 1968. *The Will to Power.* With the assistance of R. J. Hollingdale and W. A. Kaufmann. London: Weidenfeld and Nicolson.

Niv, Y., Daniel, R., Geana, A., Gershman, S. J., Leong, Y. C., Radulescu, A., and Wilson, R. C. 2015. Reinforcement Learning in Multidimensional Environments Relies on Attention Mechanisms. *The Journal of Neuroscience* 35 (21): 8145–8157. https://doi.org/10.1523/JNEUROSCI.2978-14.2015.

Nowicka, Magdalena. 2018. "I Don't Mean to Sound Racist but ... " Transforming Racism in Transnational Europe. *Ethnic and Racial Studies* 41 (5): 824–841. https://doi.org/10.1080/01419870.2017.1302093.

Nowicka, Magdalena, and Łukasz Krzyżowski. 2017.The Social Distance of Poles to Other Minorities: A Study of Four Cities in Germany and Britain. *Journal of Ethnic and Migration Studies* 43 (3): 359–378. https://doi.org/10.1080/1369183X.2016.1198253.

Obasogie, Osagie K. 2010. Do Blind People See Race? Social, Legal, and Theoretical Considerations. *Law & Society Review* 44: 585–616.

———. 2014. *Blinded by Sight: Seeing Race Through the Eyes of the Blind.* Stanford: Stanford University Press.

Orians, Gordon H. 2018. Our Biological Mind in the Modern Verbal World. In *Sensory Perceptions in Language, Embodiment and Epistemology*, eds. Annalisa Baicchi, Rémi Digonnet, and Jodi L. Sandford, 3–20. Cham: Springer.

Oyěwùmí, Oyèrónke. 1997. *The Invention of Women: Making an African Sense of Western Gender Discourses.* Minneapolis: University of Minnesota Press.

Pande, Raksha. 2017. Strategic Essentialism. In *International Encyclopedia of Geography: People, the Earth, Environment, and Technology*, 1–6. Wiley online library: Wiley.

Paraschivescu, Claudia. 2020. Experiencing Whiteness: Intra-EU Migration of Romanians to Paris and London. *Ethnic and Racial Studies* 43 (14): 2665–2683. https://doi.org/10.1080/01419870.2020.1772495.

Parrett, Matt. 2015. Beauty and the Feast: Examining the Effect of Beauty on Earnings Using Restaurant Tipping Data. *Journal of Economic Psychology* 49: 34–46. https://doi.org/10.1016/j.joep.2015.04.002.

Pauker, Kristin, Colleen M. Carpinella, David J. Lick, Diana T. Sanchez, and Kerri L. Johnson. 2018. Malleability in Biracial Categorizations: The Impact of Geographic Context and Targets' Racial Heritage. *Social Cognition* 36 (5): 461–480. https://doi.org/10.1521/soco.2018.36.5.461.

Petsko, Christopher D., and Galen V. Bodenhausen. 2020. Multifarious Person Perception: How Social Perceivers Manage the Complexity of Intersectional Targets. *Social and Personality Psychology Compass* 14 (2). https://doi.org/10.1111/spc3.12518.

Quinn, Paul C., Kang Lee, and Olivier Pascalis. 2018. Perception of Face Race by Infants: Five Developmental Changes. *Child Development Perspectives* 12 (3): 204–209. https://doi.org/10.1111/cdep.12286.

Ramsey, Jennifer L., Judith H. Langlois, and Nathan C. Marti. 2005. Infant Categorization of Faces: Ladies First. *Developmental Review* 25 (2): 212–246. https://doi.org/10.1016/j.dr.2005.01.001.

Reckwitz, Andreas. 2004. Die Gleichförmigkeit und die Bewegtheit des Subjekts: Moderne Subjektivität im Konflikt von bürgerlicher und avantgardistischer Codierung. In *Bewegung: Sozial- und kulturwissenschaftliche Konzepte*, ed. Gabriele Klein. Bielefeld: transcript.

Remedios, Jessica D., and Diana T. Sanchez. 2018. Intersectional and Dynamic Social Categories in Social Cognition. *Social Cognition* 36 (5): 453–460. https://doi.org/10.1521/soco.2018.36.5.453.

Remedios, Jessica D., and Samantha H. Snyder. 2018. The (In)Efficiency of Person Construal Involving Intersectional Social Categories. *Social Cognition* 36 (5): 517–533. https://doi.org/10.1521/soco.2018.36.5.517.

Rhodes, Gillian, Hanne C. Lie, Louise Ewing, Emma Evangelista, and James W. Tanaka. 2010. Does Perceived Race Affect Discrimination and Recognition of Ambiguous-Race Faces? A Test of the Sociocognitive Hypothesis. *Journal of Experimental Psychology. Learning, Memory, and Cognition* 36 (1): 217–223. https://doi.org/10.1037/a0017680.

Rooth, Dan-Olof. 2010. Automatic Associations and Discrimination in Hiring: Real World Evidence. *Labour Economics* 17 (3): 523–534. https://doi.org/10.1016/j.labeco.2009.04.005.

Schroer, Markus. 2019. Sociology of Attention: Fundamental Reflections on a Theoretical Program. In *The Oxford Handbook of Cognitive Sociology*, eds. Wayne H. Brekhus, and Gabe Ignatow. New York: Oxford University Press. https://doi.org/10.1093/oxfordhb/9780190273385.013.23

Searle, John R. 1996. *The Construction of Social Reality*. London: Penguin.

Shimada, Shingo. 2007. "Kulturelle Differenz und Probleme der Übersetzung." In *Zur Unüberwindbarkeit kultureller Differenz: Grundlagentheoretische Reflexionen*, eds. Jochen Dreher, and Peter Stegmaier, 113–128. Bielefeld: transcript.

Slone, Ashlyn E., John C. Brigham, and Christian A. Meissner. 2000. Social and Cognitive Factors Affecting the Own-Race Bias in Whites. *Basic and Applied Social Psychology* 22 (2): 71–84. https://doi.org/10.1207/S15324834BASP2202_1.

Smithies, Declan. 2016. Perception and the External World. *Philosophical Studies: An International Journal for Philosophy in the Analytic Tradition* 173 (4): 1119–1145.

Song, Miri. 2017. *Multiracial Parents: Mixed Families, Generational Change, and the Future of Race.* New York: New York University Press.

———. 2020. Rethinking Minority Status and 'Visibility'. *Comparative Migration Studies* 8 (1): 1–17. https://doi.org/10.1186/s40878-019-0162-2.

Spivak, Gayatri Chakravorty. 1988. Can the Subaltern Speak? In *Marxism and the Interpretation of Culture*, eds. Cary Nelson, and Lawrence Grossberg, 271–313. London: Macmillan.

Stolier, Ryan M., and Jonathan B. Freeman. 2016. Neural Pattern Similarity Reveals the Inherent Intersection of Social Categories. *Nature Neuroscience* 19 (6): 795–797. https://doi.org/10.1038/nn.4296.

Stoltz, Dustin S., and Marshall A. Taylor. 2017. Paying with Change: The Purposeful Enunciation of Material Culture. *Poetics* 64: 26–39. https://doi.org/10.1016/j.poetic.2017.07.003.

Stone, Alison. 2004. Essentialism and Anti-Essentialism in Feminist Philosophy. *The Journal of Moral Philosophy* 1 (2): 135–153. https://doi.org/10.1177/174046810400100202.

Strand, Michael, and Omar Lizardo. 2017. The Hysteresis Effect: Theorizing Mismatch in Action. *Journal of Theory of Social Behaviour* 47 (2): 164–194. https://doi.org/10.1111/jtsb.12117.

Strani, Katerina, and Anna Szczepaniak-Kozak. 2018. Strategies of Othering Through Discursive Practices: Examples from the UK and Poland. *Lodz Papers in Pragmatics* 14 (1): 163–179. https://doi.org/10.1515/lpp-2018-0008.

Strick, Madelijn, Peter F. Stoeckart, and Ap Dijksterhuis. 2015. Thinking in Black and White: Conscious Thought Increases Racially Biased Judgments through Biased Face Memory. *Consciousness and Cognition* 36: 206–218. https://doi.org/10.1016/j.concog.2015.07.001.

Strydom, Piet. 2019. Critical Theory and Cognitive Sociology. In *The Oxford Handbook of Cognitive Sociology*, eds. Wayne H. Brekhus, and Gabe Ignatow, 42–64. New York: Oxford University Press.

Suyemoto, Karen L., Micaela Curley, and Shruti Mukkamala. 2020. What Do We Mean by "Ethnicity" and "Race"? A Consensual Qualitative Research Investigation of Colloquial Understandings. *Genealogy* 4 (3): 81. https://doi.org/10.3390/genealogy4030081.

Taylor, Charles. 2007. *Modern Social Imaginaries.* Durham: Duke University Press.

Teo, Thomas, ed. 2014. *Encyclopedia of Critical Psychology.* New York: Springer.

Tereshchenko, Antonina, Alice Bradbury, and Louise Archer. 2019. Eastern European Migrants' Experiences of Racism in English Schools: Positions of Marginal Whiteness and Linguistic Otherness. *Whiteness and Education* 4 (1): 53–71. https://doi.org/10.1080/23793406.2019.1584048.

Tversky, Amos, and Daniel Kahneman. 1974. Judgment under Uncertainty: Heuristics and Biases. *Science* 185 (4157): 1124–1131. https://doi.org/10.1126/science.185.4157.1124.

Varnum, Michael E. W. 2013. What Are Lay Theories of Social Class? *PloS One* 8 (7): e70589. https://doi.org/10.1371/journal.pone.0070589.

Vetter, Petra, and Albert Newen. 2014. Varieties of Cognitive Penetration in Visual Perception. *Consciousness and Cognition* 27: 62–75. https://doi.org/10.1016/j.concog.2014.04.007.

Vincent-Lamarre, Philippe, Alexandre B. Massé, Marcos Lopes, Mélanie Lord, Odile Marcotte, and Stevan Harnad. 2016. The Latent Structure of Dictionaries. *Topics in Cognitive Science* 8 (3): 625–659. https://doi.org/10.1111/tops.12211.

Walker, Pamela, and Miles Hewstone. 2006. A Perceptual Discrimination Investigation of the Own-Race Effect and Intergroup Experience. *Applied Cognitive Psychology* 20: 41–75.

Wehrle, Maren. 2013. *Horizonte der Aufmerksamkeit: Entwurf einer dynamischen Konzeption der Aufmerksamkeit aus phänomenologischer und kognitionspsychologischer Sicht*. München: Wilhelm Fink.

Wilson, John P., Jessica D. Remedios, and Nicholas O. Rule. 2017. Interactive Effects of Obvious and Ambiguous Social Categories on Perceptions of Leadership: When Double-Minority Status May Be Beneficial. *Personality & Social Psychology Bulletin* 43 (6): 888–900. https://doi.org/10.1177/0146167217702373.

Wilson, Robert A., and Lucia Foglia. 2017. Embodied Cognition. In *The Stanford Encyclopedia of Philosophy (Spring 2017 Edition)*, ed. Edward N. Zalta. https://plato.stanford.edu/archives/spr2017/entries/embodied-cognition/.

Witherspoon, D. J., S. Wooding, A. R. Rogers, E. E. Marchani, W. S. Watkins, M. A. Batzer, and L. B. Jorde. 2007. Genetic Similarities within and between Human Populations. *Genetics* 176 (1): 351–359. https://doi.org/10.1534/genetics.106.067355.

Wojnicka, Katarzyna, and Magdalena Nowicka. 2021. Understanding Migrant Masculinities through a Spatially Intersectional Lens. *Men and Masculinities*. https://doi.org/10.1177/1097184X20986224.

Wood, Michael, Dustin Stoltz, Justin van Ness, and Marshall Taylor. 2018. Schemas and Frames. *Sociological Theory* 36 (3): 244–261.

Young, Steven G., Kurt Hugenberg, Michael J. Bernstein, and Donald F. Sacco. 2012. Perception and Motivation in Face Recognition: A Critical Review of Theories of the Cross-Race Effect. *Personality and Social Psychology Review* 16 (2): 116–142. https://doi.org/10.1177/1088868311418987.

Zerubavel, Eviatar. 2015. *Hidden in Plain Sight: The Social Structure of Irrelevance*. Oxford: Oxford University Press.

Open Access This chapter is licensed under the terms of the Creative Commons Attribution 4.0 International License (http://creativecommons.org/licenses/by/4.0/), which permits use, sharing, adaptation, distribution and reproduction in any medium or format, as long as you give appropriate credit to the original author(s) and the source, provide a link to the Creative Commons licence and indicate if changes were made.

The images or other third party material in this chapter are included in the chapter's Creative Commons licence, unless indicated otherwise in a credit line to the material. If material is not included in the chapter's Creative Commons licence and your intended use is not permitted by statutory regulation or exceeds the permitted use, you will need to obtain permission directly from the copyright holder.

CHAPTER 3

Revisualising Intersectionality: Conversations

Tiara Roxanne

Abstract Roxanne introduces the "conversations" format which combined methods of artistic research and instigated the transdisciplinary research undergirding the publication of *Revisualising Intersectionality*. Although each conversation was dedicated to one concept, namely trans*, sameness, perception, and intimacy, in the chapter, Roxanne explains how they are all positioned as epistemologies that challenge binaries (e.g., queer theory) and categorisation (e.g., critical race theory). Via readings of Doireann O'Malley's film *Prototypes* and Stephanie Comilang's sci-fi documentary *Lumapit Sa Akin, Paraiso (Come to Me, Paradise)*, Roxanne draws attention to how visuality influences the presentation of bodies across structural and societal paradigms and how our external experience is based on visual sense-making.

Keywords Intersectionality • Artistic Research • Film • Visuality

Revisualising Intersectionality emerges from a joint interest in probing artistic research methodologies and theoretical approaches that rupture binaries whilst employing the concept of intersectionality via the visual sphere. In preparation for the publication, the three authors of the book debated how the visual can dissolve certain categories and help us think across disciplines. With the overall aim to confront the constraints of categories, we sought to interpolate the visual through explorative modes of critique. That is why we explored both the collaborative and conversational forms of critique as inspired by artistic research methodologies introduced in *Artistic Research—Theories, Methods and Practices* (2005) by Mika Hannula, Juha Suoranta, and Tere Vadén. The authors propose that artistic research needs to integrate different forms of thought and expression which aid in developing new and dynamic outcomes. In order to achieve such research outcomes that open space for critical engagement, Hannula, Suoranta, and Vadén suggest that researchers develop their own research method (2014: 68). Additionally, Hannula et al. "present five approaches that can be of use when developing new methodological tools for artistic research" which are, "conversation and dialogue, analysis of media objects, collaborative case studies, ethnography and interventions, and design-based research" (2014: 68). Two approaches we wanted to implement were "conversation and dialogue" and "collaborative case studies" (Hannula et al. 2014: 68). The first is a method that takes dialectics into account, both in writing and speaking, where new "languages of critique and hope" arrive through "conversation and dialogue" (Hannula et al. 2014: 71). The second, "collaborative case studies", is an approach that insists on research developed among a group of researchers and artists alike which is exhibited in participatory activities and knowledge sharing (Hannula et al. 2014: 89). Following this lead, we instigated a series of events called "conversations" that took place in Berlin in the second half of 2019 and brought into dialogue artistic practice and critical texts to open a space for discussion among scholars, researchers, artists, and other participants on how intersectionality is imagined visually and how visual imaginaries can help understand intersectional forms of social stratification. In this way, we investigated how visuality influences the presentation of bodies across structural and societal paradigms and how we shape our external experience based on our visual sense-making.

By critically engaging with the visual sphere alongside the concept intersectionality, we intended to challenge the current discourse surrounding intersectionality from a different vantage point. Although the term was coined by Kimberlé W. Crenshaw in 1989, historically, it had been attributed to other Black women activists and scholars. These historical moments trace back to Mary Church Terrell's words on overcoming sex and race in 1904 at the International Women's Congress in Berlin as well as in 1892 when Anna J. Cooper conveyed the multiple forms of oppression Black women encounter (Hark 2019). Nevertheless, by understanding intersectionality beyond constraints of structural inequalities that emerge from social categorisation and the marginalisation of women of colour from mainstream feminism, we arrive at moments of critique that invoke multiple disciplines of praxis and thought. Such critique involves the intermingling of social science, cultural theory, and visual disciplines in order to assist in thinking about the complexities surrounding (in)visibility and categorisation, especially alongside the expansion of technology and surveillance software which significantly impacts our cognition.

As digital platforms serve as guideposts for visual exposure online, the visibility of bodies increases, asking us to think about ways in which intersectionality can address the systemic structures located within technology. We are forced to confront new layers of systemic oppression from the offline to the online space. We enter a chaotic field of "diversity and inclusion" dialogues across these systems, which is why, artistic knowledge production, visuality, and the new, digital, modes through which difference acquires meaning appeared crucial for our interrogation. Consequently, the "revis(ualis)ing intersectionality: conversations" event series approached the visual sphere as a concept to think through new inequalities and discover how we can make sense of the visibility of difference without imposing a fixed meaning of categories such as gender, race, and class. It was important to us not to conflate the concept of intersectionality with utopian fantasies of universality and inclusion but rather to use it as a conduit for non-normative ways of critically engaging with the world using the visual sphere as a starting point while implementing "conversation and dialogue" and "collaborative case studies".

The visual sphere re-presents bodies through the historical, present, and future image. The visual, as a theoretical and abstract concept, is both cognitive and embodied which impacts our identity, our sense of belonging (or feeling of sameness and community with others), and our relation to self and world. Additionally, images are affective on multiple levels regarding the cerebral, visceral, internal, and external experience. As sensing bodies are always in motion due to the external experience, the corporeal experience is affected on social (cultural), cognitive (psychoanalytical) and political levels. Bodies as sites of categorisation are re-presented in the visual sphere, imposed upon, and shaken, which prompted us to re-engage with the concept of intersectionality in relation to artistic forms such as film and performance. Since bodies are moving visual markers, as in dance or performance art, images in motion, as seen in film for example and non-static entities more generally, we must challenge forms of categorisation. By taking the collaborative and the conversation space between researchers and artists, we sought to examine visuality and intersectionality from four distinct perspectives.

Although each conversation was dedicated to one concept, namely trans*, sameness, perception, and intimacy, they were all positioned as epistemologies that challenge binaries (e.g., queer and transgender theory) and categorisation (e.g., critical race theory). As most disciplines have sought to find a relation between intersectionality and their own trajectory by illustrating how a particular methodology situates intersectionality in accordance with named discipline, each conversation within this series of events brought together multiple disciplinary angles and methodologies to serve as a basis for questioning. Each section below addresses the epistemology of the conversation more thoroughly by describing the event, the terms that were discussed, and what was presented visually in more detail.

Trans*

Cinema is a medium that captures bodies through the moving image. In this way, the body becomes a vector of passage. As the reproduced image fuels affect and intention, generally the body responds to the environment and creates meaning of self and others. The narrative encompassing the body or the bodies within the film reproduces various encounters of meaning. The filmic body expands into the multitude. This kind of corporeal conversion prompted us to ask how intersectionality, cinematic representation, and queer theory converge towards a critique that works to deconstruct social and cultural structures that uphold binaries by looking at the moving image (cinema) with the trans* body as a site of passage.

For this conversation entitled trans*, we choose to view Doireann O'Malley's film *Prototypes*, which "explores new perspectives on trans identity through the lens of a post psychoanalytic, schizo-analytic methodology, entangling rhizomatic forms of thought, systems theory, consciousness, machine learning and quantum transformation" (O'Malley 2018). The film, more specifically, focuses on transgender female to male identity and transition processes, community, kinship, as well as otherworldly science fiction-esque realms. Throughout the film, we are taken on a journey of architecturally stark landscapes, dreamscapes which involve Jungian conversations. These conversations seem to carry a desire to uncover the unconscious world of being in a trans* body and overall utopian visions for trans* community, sexuality, and general beingness to exist and expand into. The film allows us to think outside of categorisation, beyond the binary, and more imaginatively when it comes to trans* bodies and cinema. The film, as such, confronts the binaries societal structures forced onto bodies which allows for a merging between intersectionality, film as a visual medium, and the trans* body as the moment from which we explore questions and discussions inspired by the preliminary text for this first conversation.

Prior to the conversation, participants read "Cinematic/Trans*/Bodies Now (and Then, and to Come)" by Cáel M. Keegan, Laura Horak, and Eliza Steinbock, a building block approach to the screening of Doireann O'Malley's *Prototypes*. We wanted to provide a text that asked us to enquire about tensions the trans* body and visual representations carry within cinema. The *Somatechnics* article by Keegan et al. describes somatechnical approaches as ways in which "cinematic experiences might transition bodies in characteristically trans* modes of wayward gendering, inspired by definitions of transgender as 'a movement across a socially imposed boundary away from an unchosen starting place'" (2018: 2). The term somatechnics used here in relation to trans* cinema and bodies, provides space for expansion, multiplicity, and non-linearity. We learn that somatechnics, according to Keegan et al., is about "building spaces where such new and transmuted filed formations might come together" (2018: 3) falling in line with the exploratory vision of the conversations format.

Additionally, we learn that the term somatechnics emerges from the desire for a "balance with trans* as a way to move newly among times and spaces, across fields and forms, toward (im)possible sensations, affects, and futures—always rooted in the material realities of transgender life as it has been historically and bodily constituted" (Keegan et al. 2018: 3). Moreover, we explored trans* as explained by Jack Halberstam, who reminds us that "trans* can be a name for expansive forms of difference, haptic relations of knowing, uncertain modes of being, and the disaggregation of identity politics predicated upon the separating out of many kinds of experience that actually blend together, intersect and mix" (2018: 5). The coalescing of Halberstam's notion on trans*, somatechnics, and O'Malley's *Prototypes*, prompted participants to meditate on the trans* body via representation, visualisation, and the multiple meanings and prospects that unfold within the cinematic space.

One metaphor participants spoke of was the images of architectural structures and their relation to the trans* body. Throughout the film, the analogy of architecture is seen as a structure and a body. As we move from the isolated tall houses and square stark window frames to nature, we engage with the preconceived notion of architectural and bodily functionalities, limitations, and possibilities of conversion. We are also forced to think about the shift from nature to the artificial online spaces as a moment of modification regarding the body and how it digitally transmits as well.

In the film, the camera moves between durational moments of predefined spaces such as windows, buildings, and landscapes, making a connection to pre-determined gender roles. And as the camera continues to move through these shape-shifting spaces, the notion of predetermination is challenged. The moving images of rooms and structures going through the building and unbuilding process are a clear parallel to the trans* body. Consequently, Halberstam's work regarding transition and functionality guided this part of the evening's discussion on how architecture, or space more generally, and transness converge and dissect the binary.

Not only is there a hybridity between architectural structures and the corporeal, time within the film is also exhibited non-linearly. Between the durational shots, the conversations between individuals and the psychoanalyst and the community gatherings (Fig. 3.1), time becomes unknown. The architectural images and bodies become thresholds that are transitive and mouldable, like time travelling on bodies, within bodies and beyond bodies. Additionally, the dialogues between the psychoanalyst and the

Fig. 3.1 Doireann O'Malley, *Prototypes* film still

individuals, though they differ in character and details which are shared, shed light on histories of experience with anti-trans violence but also brought forward the possibility of a utopia in another dimension.

Towards the end of the film, we see the protagonist interact with a portal, which is physically imagined as a mirror, perhaps a vision of the multiverse and a departure. As the protagonist stands in front of the portal, we enter the multiverse, both a quantum space and syntax, or perhaps even the void (Fig. 3.2). A space where syntax and the grammar of the (trans*) body no longer exist—a utopia. In other words, we move from the architecture and nature analogy through forming of the unconscious to semiotics of trans* and utopia. Thereafter, trans* semiotics moves from the material world into other dimensions that are non-linear. The film's re-presentation of architecture and bodies asks us to think beyond or across gender normativity by creating an environment of malleable structures and transitioning bodies, both together and separate, inviting or even romanticising utopia, as a physical elsewhere or other space in the science-fiction scenario of the film.

Trans*, as our first conversation, set the scene for our next conversation, sameness. Sameness took our previous engagement with cinema but with an aim to interpolate the meaning of being like one another, being together and the visual presentations of each character and the lives they lead.

Fig. 3.2 Doireann O'Malley, *Prototypes* film still

Sameness

> Despite decades of feminist theorizing on the question of difference, difference continues to be 'difference from,' that is, the difference from 'white woman.' Distinct from a frame that privileges 'difference within,' 'difference from' produces difference as a contradiction rather than as a recognizing it as a perpetual and continuous process of splitting. (Puar 2012: 53)

As Jasbir Puar criticises the duality of intersectionality via its relationship with difference, but not with sameness, our second conversation was dedicated to moving beyond the framework of difference and interest in what Puar calls "splitting" (2012: 53). Additionally, moving towards the process of thinking through ways in which visuality proposes conceptions of sameness was core to this conversation.

Since categories enact frameworks of difference according to varying identifiers, sameness must also play an important role with regard how to revis(ualis)e intersectionality. In addition to examining similarities in behaviour, identity, and marginalisation, sameness also implies shared experience and connection between the self and others. Some of our questions were: how can we view sameness without the binary of difference, if intersectionality relates to difference by way of categorisation and the separation implied therein, how can we also usefully employ it to interrogate sameness?

For this conversation, we screened Filipina-Canadian filmmaker Stephanie Comilang's *Lumapit Sa Akin, Paraiso* (*Come to Me, Paradise*), which is a science fiction documentary set in Hong Kong (Fig. 3.3). The sci-fi film documents the lives of three migrant Filipina domestic workers who are subject to forced labour, exploitation, and human trafficking. As a result, these injustices are shared between them and displayed in their individual and collective routines. Furthermore, most of the footage is displayed through the lens of an omnipresent drone called Paradise. Throughout the film, we experience the disheartening circumstances the women encounter, but also share with one another.

Prior to the screening, participants read "Black Cyberfeminism: Ways forward for Intersectionality and Digital Sociology" by Tressie McMillan Cottom (2016). McMillan Cottom's text examines the unequal power relations within digital spaces, highlighting the vulnerability Black women experience through forms of hypervisibility and algorithmic stratification online. Furthermore, the text explores "what intersectionality brings to

Fig. 3.3 Stephanie Comilang, *Lumapit Sa Akin, Paraiso (Come to Me, Paradise)* film still

digital sociology" (McMillan Cottom 2016: 211). She describes how digital sociology observes, "social processes at the micro, meso, and macro level(s) that are mediated by digital logics, technologies, and platforms" (McMillan Cottom 2016: 211). Though McMillan Cottom's examination dives into an analysis of Black women's vulnerabilities online and the structural inequalities therein, we were able to apply the concept of digital sociology on all three levels within the film. From the perspective of the drone, Paradise, we experience the domestic worker's daily lives individually and collectively on micro, meso, and macro levels.

The drone, Paradise, is a technological tool that is used to narrate and capture the lives of the women workers in the film. In this way, through the gaze of Paradise, we experience how the women share a sense of sameness. Throughout the film, we are shown various scenes of the women participating in different rituals together. In one scene, the women dance in formation with one another. Another scene displays the women sharing food and conversation in open spaces throughout the city. Both scenes highlight a kind of harmony experienced between the women when they are together, a kind of sameness outside of their labour as domestic workers (Fig. 3.4). Consequently, in the conversation, we discussed how the domestic female workers in the film are made the "same" in relation to

Fig. 3.4 Stephanie Comilang, *Lumapit Sa Akin, Paraiso (Come to Me, Paradise)* film still

their employers, their wardrobes, as well as in their daily routines with work and socialising and how Paradise might influence this. Each of their routines and shared experiences are social practices exhibited on micro and meso levels. The women come together for community, sharing and dancing forming community. At the same time, the women remain unseen, socially unrecognised, and marginalised reduced to a fixed identity as migrant domestic workers. On a macro level, this quality of having a fixed identity is presented by Paradise's pervasive surveying as meditated through digitisation.

With its omnipresence, the drone's gaze emphasises the influence digital technologies have on the social processes of the women in the film. Because we experience the women's lives through the gaze of Paradise, we are provided with different perspectives regarding their routines and the way they share a sense of sameness. In addition to narrating the film, Paradise also serves as the channel of communication the domestic workers use to transmit their messages back home. We see the women taking photos and video messages to send to their families (Fig. 3.3). Thus, the women use Paradise as a medium of communication and connection. These methods of communication reinforce digital modes of data collection. By digitising their memories and sending them back to their families, they form a database of entangled images and data, contributing to the macro level of big data. Big data here symbolises a digital form of sameness, a large collection of images, messages, and videos.

The social and digital practices of the women nearly collapse into one through the lens of Paradise. We do not experience one without the other. As our second conversation, sameness investigated connectivity outside of categorisation within the medium of film. As the women shared rituals and routines outside of their domestic work, they enforced modes of sameness beyond the confines of categorisation as domestic workers. Their embodied practices disrupt categorisation based on their migration and work status and include communal and creative practices that extend into the realm of the digital, thereby also blurring the boundaries between creative use on the micro levels and surveillance practices on the macro level of global digital technologies and migration regimes. The visual representation of their lives does address intersectional modes of oppression that female domestic workers face but it also extends again into a creative utopian collective mode of producing your own images, sharing connection across space via video and dance. For the third conversation, we moved more towards the performative and physical avenues for exploring the visual and the intersectional.

Perception

Cognitive science tells us that our ways of understanding each other is influenced by how we understand ourselves. This kind of epistemology of self and other, as experienced through perception, largely relies on the visual, on what is (in)visible and how that visual information is perceived by us. Furthermore, perception interrogates how visual information guides our actions in interacting with others as well as the environment. For the third conversation, we turned to perception to explore the psychological and social processes we experience when seeing and perceiving ourselves and others.

Because perception is multifaceted with regard to the visual, we integrated a more performative and physical medium in this conversation. We wanted to shift the focus from film to a more embodied form of epistemology. There were two moving parts to this conversation which included an explorative talk by Ashkan Sepahvand and live illustration by Nine Yamamoto-Masson. The combination of Sepahvand's talk and Yamamoto-Masson's drawing created an immediacy of information, expanding the discussion space into an artistic practice along with exploration of texts and visual media. The atmosphere was continually shifting our own perceptions, with participants at times sitting still and at times moving between the front and the back of the room where the speaker and artist were situated.

Ashkan Sepahvand led a talk on his current artistic research project on the AIDS crisis (Fig. 3.5). Sepahvand is interested in developing a queer critique of political visibility, suggesting instead an aesthetics of the (in)visible and a politics of (dis)appearance. His talk asked the following questions: what does it mean to be seen, who is doing the looking, what are the risks of showing? (Sepahvand 2019). During the conversation, we engaged with voice, sound, and text, specifically reading from Larry Mitchell's *The Faggots and Their Friends between Revolutions* published in 1977. Sepahvand stated, "as positions that evade or refuse representation, transparency, clarity, and understanding, I am interested in how these instead propose the visionary, sensory, imaginary, and mysterious as modalities for queer knowledge-(un)making" (2019). Throughout his talk,

Fig. 3.5 Ashkan Sepahvand, 27.11.2019, photo by Charlotte de Bekker

participants read from Mitchell's text, walked through and navigated the space with their bodies, challenging new forms of perception.

In addition to Sepahvand's interdisciplinary work, Yamamoto-Masson's live drawings also engaged with the sensory. As seen below, the drawing displays faces with the words "become ungovernable" (Fig. 3.6). One might perceive that Yamamoto-Masson is questioning un/seenness and (in)visibility but also the idea that means of social control rely on the (hyper)visibility of certain populations.

Our third conversation asked us to think more experientially. Sepahvand's talk highlighted that perception is a relation, where agency extends beyond the visual. And Nine Yamamoto-Masson's live drawings encountered the space by taking the room of moving bodies into account and illustrating various drawings alongside the participants' exploration of the room. The discourse between the two became a perceptual echo. The final conversation, intimacy, also addressed the performative and experimental.

Fig. 3.6 Illustration by Nine Yamamoto-Masson, 27.11.2019, photo by Charlotte de Bekker

Intimacy

Digital technologies promote hypervisibility of our bodies, as presented online, which shapes our relations, our intimacies. Where we might mutually recognise a shared togetherness within the digital sphere, we might also inhabit a feeling of isolation, or even seduction. We are intimate with the digital; the data that is collected about us and by us is a form of intimacy. Our relationship with digital technology moulds how we mediate intimacy.

For our final conversation, we wanted to investigate the concept of intimacy as an unfolding form of oppression and/or togetherness through the performative and artistic as mediums of expression. With the increased inclusion of digital technologies in our daily experience, our understanding of intimacy shifts. Lauren Berlant reminds us that intimacy is a complicated narrative. Berlant explains:

> To intimate is to communicate with the sparest of signs and gestures, and at its root, intimacy has the quality of eloquence and brevity. But intimacy also involves an aspiration for a narrative about something shared, a story about both oneself and others that will turn out in a particular way. (1998: 281)

As intimacy expands our narratives and relation to others, with others, which is only intensified by digital technologies, we were curious in thinking about intimacy as a way of experiencing or seeing intersectionality. Intimacy as a relation between body and digitality, between digital bodies and digitality. Some questions we asked were, how does the growing implementation of digital technologies in our daily lives, and the inescapability therein, shape our encounter(s) with intimacy?

This conversation was led by a talk from Shaka McGlotten whose work focuses on anthropology and art, combining Black studies and queer theory, to consider new media technologies. Their talk discussed the algorithmic intimacies tied to streaking, which is a "term used to describe forms of gamified sociability that emerged from social media apps like Snapchat where streaking refers to ongoing and uninterrupted series of exchanges. The point is to keep the streak alive" (McGlotten 2019). Streaking within the digital manipulates ways in which we intimate with one another regarding what we share of ourselves and with whom and the responses we receive. It becomes an endless feedback loop with intimacy at its core of questioning and commanding that we confront the digital identity we are building online of ourselves in relation to others and the intersectional modes of being perceived as an identity online.

After McGlotten's talk, Zander Porter and James Batchelor performed an "embodied interrelation" titled "Alien Intimacy" (2019). Porter and Batchelor described their performance as "a dance of 'human' and 'alien' embodiments" which "speculates on the movement of an interpersonally constructed alien sense, conjuring the connection for the visible and the invisible or the physically embodied and the virtually disembodied" (Batchelor and Porter 2019). The performance between the two of them displayed a kind of intimacy that lies between two bodies, when two bodies are close but do not touch, the "almost touchable" (Batchelor and Porter 2019). Covered in silver paint, matching black tops, and blue accented shorts, the duo performed a dance on stage sharing a small space (Fig. 3.7). The choreography exhibited many movements between Batchelor and Porter moving towards one another without touching, jumping up and down or circling the stage, highlighting the negative space between the bodies which became a form of intimacy. These choreographed gestures break down and break out of the confines of the assumption which tells us intimacy must include touch. Here, the choreography is an embodied gesture of intimacy shared between the two showing us that intimacy does not need to include touch (Fig. 3.8).

The conversation that followed amongst Shaka McGlotten, Zander Porter, James Batchelor, the participants, and me covered many different concerns inspired by both the talk and performance (Fig. 3.9). Many questions and responses explored intimacy and intersectionality from different perspectives often connected to the feeling of alienation. Because intersectionality is deeply tied to identity politics and the way in which we navigate from our own subjectivities, we often feel alien to ourselves. We are constantly perceiving ourselves through the perspective of the other, materially (labour forces, friends, family, e.g.), and digitally (the algorithm, data mining practices, e.g.). Often this view obscures our reality enforcing a feeling of isolation, rather than intimacy. Online, we are tied to digitally static identities due to the constraints of the algorithm, the data that is collected about us and the output we are given online through advertisements for example, asks us to find new ways that help us break out of stasis and experience intimacy. Thereby, we might investigate ways in which different forms of artistic expression like dance and performance might be gestural responses to the feeling of alienation exacerbated by technology (e.g., data mining, the algorithm, the streak).

Fig. 3.7 James Batchelor & Zander Porter perform "Alien Intimacy", 19.12.2019, photo by Charlotte de Bekker

Fig. 3.8 Zander Porter, 19.12.2019, photo by Charlotte de Bekker

Thereafter, we debated how touch transforms the meaning of intimacy with regard to technology of haptics and how we literally touch and use our phones. One might argue that we are more intimate with our smartphone than with each other. The conversation did not stop at (non)touch and technology, it expanded into more discussion about the vulnerabilities of QBIPOC experience in digital spheres and the different forms of

Fig. 3.9 Shaka McGlotten, Tiara Roxanne, James Batchelor, and Zander Porter, 19.12.2019, photo by Charlotte de Bekker

intimacy that might transpire on social media platforms. We discussed how technology amplifies hypervisibility of QBIPOC bodies due to surveillance and data mining extraction and asked questions of finding and creating safe online spaces to be in with other QBIPOC. Finally, we closed the conversation acknowledging that communication is also a form intimacy, which can be explored in offline and online spaces.

Conclusion

Each conversation considered two of the five approaches introduced by Hannula et al.: "conversation and dialogue" and "collaborative case studies" (2014: 68). By taking these two approaches and pairing them with a different concept, we discovered "new languages of critique and hope" (Hannula et al. 2014: 71), providing different vantage points regarding intersectionality and the visual sphere. From trans*, where we arrived at notions about the malleability of the body and how this malleability changes given the gaze through which we view a body and how this gaze can be shifted from the confines of heteronormativity in trans utopian cinematic representation. For sameness, we explored cinema once again but through the "eyes" of the drone and learned about sameness as embodied conviviality (rituals, dance, ceremony) as opposed to the categories of identity that intersectionality highlights (race, class, gender). Our conversation on perception extended the more physical dimension of perception by pairing Sepahvand's talk with Yamamoto-Masson's live drawing. We shifted our perceptions by exploring the collaborative research methodology more specifically in relation to communal reading practices and visual representation. And our final conversation blended a lecture and a performance that explored new forms of intimacy online and offline, especially between BIPOC. Each different outcome provided us with more questions about intersectionality's relationship with the visual sphere. Since intersectionality provides a platform to ask questions about how to think across categories, using artistic research methods alongside the titular concepts for each conversation, we formed new critiques regarding the un/seen and hypervisibility more generally. Bringing in these different approaches showed us that conversation is much more than a verbal dialogue but also a collaboration.

WORKS CITED

FILMS:

Doireann O'Malley, dir. *Prototypes*. 2018.
Stephanie Comilang, dir. *Lumapit Sa Akin, Paraiso*. 2016.

LECTURES:

McGlotten, Shaka. 2019, December 19. *Algorithmic Intimacies*. Lecture presented at Revis(ualis)ing Intersectionality: A Series of Conversations: Pt. 4, intimacy in Südblock, Berlin.
Sepahvand, Ashkan. 2019, November 27. *What does it mean to be seen, who is doing the looking, what are the risks of showing?* Lecture presented at Revis(ualis)ing Intersectionality: A Series of Conversations: Pt. 3, perception in DeZIM-Institute, Berlin.

PERFORMANCES:

Batchelor, James, & Porter, Zander (Dancers). 2019, December 19. *Alien Intimacy*. Live performance in Südblock, Berlin.

TEXTS:

Berlant, Lauren. 1998. Intimacy: A Special Issue. *Critical Inquiry* 24 (2): 281–288. https://doi.org/10.1086/448875.
Crenshaw, Kimberlé. 1989. Demarginalizing the Intersection of Race and Sex: A Black Feminist Critique of Antidiscrimination Doctrine, Feminist Theory and Antiracist Politics. *University of Chicago Legal Forum* 1989 (1): 139–167.
Halberstam, Jack. 2018. *Trans*: A Quick and Quirky Account of Gender Variability*. Oakland: University of California Press.
Hannula, Mika, Juha Suoranta, and Tere Vadén. 2014. *Artistic Research Methodology: Narrative, Power and the Public*. New York: Peter Lang.
Hark, Sabine. 2019. "Intersectionality—a Weighty Concept with History." Heinrich-Böll-Stiftung Gunda-Werner-Institut Feminism and Gender Democracy. Accessed October 15, 2020. https://www.gwi-boell.de/en/2019/05/20/intersectionality-weighty-concept-history.
Keegan, Cáel M., Laura Horak, and Eliza Steinbock. 2018. Cinematic/Trans*/Bodies Now (and Then, and to Come). *Somatechnics* 8 (1): 1–13. https://doi.org/10.3366/soma.2018.0233.

McMillan Cottom, Tressie. 2016. Black Cyberfeminism: Ways forward for Intersectionality and Digital Sociology. In *Digital Sociologies*, eds. Jessie Daniels, Karen Gregory, and Tressie McMillan Cottom, 211–231. Bristol: Bristol University Press.

Mitchell, Larry, and Ned Asta (drawings). *The Faggots and Their Friends between Revolutions*. New York: Calamus, 1977.

Puar, Jasbir K. 2012. 'I Would Rather Be a Cyborg Than a Goddess': Becoming-Intersectional in Assemblage Theory. *philoSOPHIA: A Journal of Continental Feminism* 2 (1): 49–66.

Open Access This chapter is licensed under the terms of the Creative Commons Attribution 4.0 International License (http://creativecommons.org/licenses/by/4.0/), which permits use, sharing, adaptation, distribution and reproduction in any medium or format, as long as you give appropriate credit to the original author(s) and the source, provide a link to the Creative Commons licence and indicate if changes were made.

The images or other third party material in this chapter are included in the chapter's Creative Commons licence, unless indicated otherwise in a credit line to the material. If material is not included in the chapter's Creative Commons licence and your intended use is not permitted by statutory regulation or exceeds the permitted use, you will need to obtain permission directly from the copyright holder.

CHAPTER 4

The Ends of Visibility

Elahe Haschemi Yekani

Abstract Following an introduction to the field of visual culture studies and the idea of revisualising intersectionality, Haschemi Yekani draws on different forms of media use, artistic practice, and everyday visual culture to problematise notions of difference that rely on a binary of invisibility and visibility. Haschemi Yekani argues that the question of in/visibility needs to go beyond superficially diverse representation and also concerns technological development and a reflection of how media operate within global postcolonial networks of capital. Via discussions of "colour blindness" and "bathroom panic", the chapter reflects the potential of artistic practice to contribute to a queering and transing of identification and the image repertoire. This includes post-representational artistic practice, strategies of disidentification as well as forms of refusing representation altogether.

Keywords Intersectionality • Visual culture • Visuality • Transgender • Colour blindness • Post-representational art

Visual Culture and Intersectionality

Perceptions of visual difference and similarity are not always straightforward, and we must not confuse the mere presence of something with its visibility. As Magdalena Nowicka explains in greater detail in Chap. 2 in which she asks where difference begins, to understand perceptibility, we need to engage with the process of foregrounding certain aspects while delegating others to the background, that is, the constant (and necessary) filtering mechanisms we employ to make sense of our surroundings. In this context, Nowicka introduces the work of Eviatar Zerubavel who uses "visibility and invisibility as metaphors for *relevance* and *irrelevance*" (2015: 6) and draws our attention to the famous ambiguous example of Rubin's Vase emblematising the "figure-and-ground model" in which viewers can recognise two different shapes in the same image but not simultaneously. When looking at pictures of this kind, "We can thus perceive either the vase or the faces, but not both of them at once, together" (Zerubavel 2015: 16). However, as Zerubavel himself concedes, the relationship between remarkability and unremarkability, what is noticed and what is not, is already implicated within cultural norms and power dynamics. To make this point, he briefly mentions the construction of Blackness in the US context, as the "visibility" of African ancestry, as opposed to the unremarkable absence of such ancestry when it comes to the constructions of whiteness (2015: 23). In the introduction to this volume, we also highlight that the realm of visual culture, and specifically artistic image production, can be disruptive to visually naturalised forms of social inequality. When we discussed the Rubin Vase example during one of our transdisciplinary workshops that preceded this publication, I was immediately reminded of the work of US-American artist Kara Walker who is famous for her adaptation of the silhouette which likewise utilises stark black and white contrasts. These black cut-out figures against a white background became popular as "shadow portraits" in the late eighteenth and early nineteenth century and were often associated with women's handicraft. The term "shadow portrait" highlights that the depicted faces were the black shadow of a supposedly white counterfeit. Walker recontextualises this technique by depicting the disturbing realities of sexualised violence but also sexual agency in grotesque figures. Reproducing crass contrasts between the racialised carnality of the systematic abuse of Black bodies, especially female bodies, under chattel slavery, Walker renders visible the brutality of enslavement that the supposedly genteel planter class engaged in and conveniently overlooked as the shadowy background that still haunts contemporary society and which Christina Sharpe describes as "monstrous intimacies" (2010: 153–187). The visible two-dimensional blackness of the shadow is linked to the complex embodied experience of racialisation and demonstrates that race is both inextricably tied to visibility and yet exceeds the realm of the visual. The supposed physiognomic markers of race are exaggerated in the figures and the visual representation of "colour" is flattened to the binary of the black paper against a white background which lacks a "real" referent. We can distinguish white from Black figures in her installation despite both being represented in the black cut-out (and there are also inverted versions of white cut-outs against a black background). Accordingly, the spectacle of racialised violence is immediately graspable in these depictions, precisely because the artworks adapt the crude mechanisms of the racist binary sorting and segregation of people. Engaging with this aesthetic technique, film scholar Alessandra Raengo describes Walker's practice as follows:

> while the shadow is a fleeting indexical sign, because it requires the presence of the body that produces it, the silhouette is its human-made, durable reproduction and as such survives the body's departure. In the silhouette the body has fully vacated the sign—dissolved in the abstract iconicity of its contour—and has left behind a blackness, which is held as the trace of its past presence and current absence. (Raengo 2016: online)

As a shape, blackness is both linked to the representation of the body and abstracted from it—our ability to see, to understand the intersectional and historically as well as geographically distinct meanings of visually encoded racialised difference is both superficial and phenomenological, it is linked to how the cultural image repertoire[1] impacts lived experiences, or, again in Raengo's vocabulary of film analysis, through Walker's artwork, we can understand Blackness as "the meeting point between the screen and the skin" (Raengo 2016: online).

While visuality cannot be reduced to individual perception, it is, of course, interrelated with both vision and embodiment. Visuality is reliant on perception as a social and cognitive process but conversely also affects how difference is individually comprehended and socially communicated (Obasogie 2014: 50; Dikovitskaya 2005: 9, cf. also Chap. 2). Accordingly, when we talk about visuality and the perception of sameness/difference in this book, we do not mean to evoke the alleged visual evidentiality of Western ocular-centrism or objectivity,[2] and it is important to note that sight is not the only sensorial sphere through which difference and sameness are perceived or experienced. But while our project might risk an over-emphasis on vision at the expense of other senses, we also believe that social recognition is tied to a privileged role of visual representation. Western knowledge production but also emancipatory political projects have strongly relied on metaphors of seeing as recognition. In this way, visuality is immediately sutured to questions of visibility *as* representation. However, as Johanna Schaffer (2008) emphasises, we should not simply confuse more visibility with social recognition and not prematurely equate visuality and visibility. To clarify some of these distinctions, it is helpful to retrace how these terms originated and continue to be critically interrogated in the academic field of visual culture studies.

The beginning of what is now known as visual culture (studies) emerged from the wish to infuse traditional methodologies of art history with a post-foundational critique that set out to challenge "the figure of the observer who is nominally a free sovereign" (Crary 1988: 33) and gained prominence more widely in the 1990s. Hal Foster introduces visuality as a term that, while not in binary opposition to the physiological notion of vision, does refer to the ways in which scopic regimes[3] are shaped by historical power relations. He writes,

> Although vision suggests sight as a physical operation, and visuality sight as a social fact, the two are not opposed as nature to culture: vision is social and historical too, and visuality involves the body and the psyche. Yet neither are they identical: here, the difference between the terms signals a difference within the visual—between the mechanism of sight and its historical techniques, between the datum of vision and its discursive determinations—a difference, many differences, among how we see, how we are able, allowed, or made to see, and how we see this seeing or the unseen therein. With its own rhetoric and representations, each scopic regime seeks to close out these differences: to make of its many social visualities one essential vision, or to order them in a natural hierarchy of sight. (Foster 1988: ix)

Correspondingly, visual culture studies explores how socio-cultural visuality is translated into (hierarchical) visibility and what is sometimes referred to as the cultural grammar of vision (cf. Brighenti 2010: 23).[4] Resulting from this interest in the links between aesthetics, media, and power dynamics, visual culture further took its cues from studies on the so-called male gaze in narrative cinema (Mulvey 1989) and the racialised "spectacle of the 'Other'" in mass media (Hall 1997). It is therefore not a coincidence that many of the foundational works in visual culture studies discuss the representation of women and racialised minorities.[5] In this framework, visuality describes the historical/cultural signifying practices by which meanings are visually communicated and which are themselves implicated in how media operate. Accordingly, the concept of visuality is concerned with how the representation of bodies and the concomitant construction of identities and groups inform the circulation of images within networks that are shaped by hierarchical power relations.[6]

In his study on *Visibility in Social Theory and Social Research* Andrea Mubi Brighenti further elaborates on the distinction between visuality and visibility and on how vision and epistemology are intertwined in various disciplines. Brighenti offers a much more systematic overview of how these terms are used in various academic contexts than I am capable of here. He defines "visibility as a phenomenon that is inherently ambiguous, highly dependent upon contexts and complex social, technical and political arrangements which could be termed 'regimes' of visibility" (Brighenti 2010: 3). In this understanding, visuality is framed broadly as "the cultural counterpart of the sense of sight" and visibility is proposed to denote "a dimension of the social at large, unrestricted to the visual domain" (Brighenti 2010: 3, 4). Social visibility is therefore reliant on, but also exceeds the realm of visual representation. This notion of visibility is also relevant for our efforts to revis(ualis)e intersectionality as it corresponds to an interest in the social effects of visual perception and the manner in which these are intertwined with the cultural image repertoire. To put it differently, technology, media, and vision can be understood as different (but interlinked) spheres that impact the microlevel of individual perceptions of sameness and difference as well as the macrolevel of systemic distinctions that give rise to social inequalities.

While we criticise certain aspects of how visual representation and recognition are sometimes conflated, we are, as mentioned in the introduction (cf. Chap. 1), certainly not invested in a banal *un*seeing of difference—quite the opposite. Part of intersectional thinking is an awareness of the social effects of perceptions of difference to achieve a more equitable and just society by tackling perceptual biases and overcoming structural discriminations. Such forms of marginalisation are often experienced precisely as the unacknowledging or even unintelligibility[7] of specific needs or lacking (political) representation, which cannot be reduced to, but includes the circulation of images in the media. W.J.T. Mitchell, who coined the term "the pictorial turn", problematises the interrelations between images, objects, and media and describes pictures themselves as "complex assemblages of virtual, material and symbolic elements" (2005: xiiv). Hence, the idea of "positive images" to counter discrimination fails to adequately capture the intricacy of how visual representation and social visibility are connected. This correlation cannot be reduced to a linear model of representation automatically begetting greater inclusivity or diversity. To bring into conversation the fields of intersectionality research and visual culture then, we need to be aware of the complexities of how images operate and how they might influence the tenuous relationship of categorisation and identification.

To combine insights from these different fields implies a certain scepticism of the usefulness of identity and fixed categories as analytical lenses. Instead, this approach requires a more pronounced focus on affects and relationalities whilst maintaining a sustained intersectional critique of power relations and the material effects these have on individuals and groups. For this purpose, seeing itself (rather than the more stable notion of representation) needs to be politicised. We wish to disrupt the idea that to see is already to know and rather understand seeing itself as a creative practice. The visual sphere offers numerous ways to aesthetically challenge viewing conventions in artistic practice,[8] but it also influences mundane affective interactions, including, of course, powerful modes of surveillance[9] and exclusion that are ingrained, for example, in social media. In the context of surveillance and digital media, recognition is no longer (or not only) an act of bestowing social acknowledgement but necessarily bound up with "coarse social sorting according to visible somatic features" (Brighenti 2010: 164). This supposed visual evidentiality of (binary) difference (re)emerges from a history of violence that has shaped colonialist knowledge production based on sorting people into racialised categories. As Denise Ferreira da Silva argues, "order involves a formulation of difference that centres visibility and presupposes and reproduces vertical and horizontal un/equality" (Silva 2011: 142). Therefore, we need to ask how one can combine a postcolonial/decolonial critique of (visual) categorisation that is prevalent in critical visuality studies with intersectionality's interest in social justice.

Part of the problem of visuality in relation to discrimination is that there is frequently a convergence of "invisibility" (as a lack of political representation) and "hypervisibility" (as being especially vulnerable to forms of violence or discriminatory policies). This dilemma has become more and more apparent, for instance, in the simultaneity of greater trans visibility in the media and the ongoing violence against trans people that is aggravated by intersectional forms of discrimination, such as racism, harassment at the workplace/economic precarity, access to health care, and/or legal status.[10] Emphasising relationality as part of intersectionality

Patricia Hill Collins and Sirma Bilge, effectively propose to think of intersectionality not as an "*either/or* binary thinking" but as a "*both/and* frame" (2016: 27). It is not helpful to discern individual aspects of discrimination but to comprehend anti-trans violence as resulting from and being intensified by the very ways in which these various modes of oppression are already entangled. In the context of intersectionality research, the reference to identities and groups appears to be an obvious starting point. But we should also factor in that there are ways in which the failure to be legible *within* identity categories is often the very result of intersectional discrimination. Not only are trans women of colour, as mentioned, precariously situated within normative gender orders, Black cis women are also frequently perceived as "ungendered" or less feminine.[11] In this case, sexism and racism do not simply "intersect" within the visual metaphor; indeed, normative notions of femininity are already informed by whiteness, heteronormativity, and perceptions of able-bodiedness in ways that exclude certain bodies from the category of "woman" to begin with. This, once more, is not to dismiss the usefulness of a relational intersectional description of these processes of discrimination, but it obliges us to find other vocabularies of analytical description. Simply treating distinct categories such as gender, race, and class as self-evident overlooks the fact that these categories are a result of the *processes* of racism and sexism, and not their origin. The sphere of the visual proves vital in understanding how these terms acquire meaning and, accordingly, we should not reduce the question of visuality to a form of mimetic political representation.

In this spirit, the term "revis(ualis)ing"—in its double meaning of revising and visualising—is used here as a heuristic tool to describe modes of seeing differently, as an attempt to intervene into normative visual orders and as a productive revision of intersectional analytics. To return once more to the issue of anti-trans violence: Trans activists and artists, whose work I will discuss in more detail later in the chapter, are adamant that a form of liberal inclusion into the codes of mainstream media representation does not automatically result in greater freedoms for trans people. Instead, what is required is a more fundamental intervention into the functioning of intelligibility, which is also linked to the idea of transing (cf. Stryker et al. 2008) the image repertoire. Much like an understanding of reading and writing as a form of storytelling that disrupts notions of scientific objectivity (Haraway 1989: 15; Hartman 2008), we should be open to more speculative ways of exploring visual representations of sameness and difference. The very term "speculation" disrupts the supposedly evidentiary relation between seeing and knowing.[12] It was initially used to describe the visual observation of the stars, but speculation also refers to reasoning that is open to surprise.[13] Revis(ualis)ing implies such an openness in challenging the terms of analysis that we employ in intersectionality research.

Having introduced both visual culture studies and the proposal to link this field more explicitly to questions of intersectionality via the heuristic tool of "revis(ualis)ing", in the following sections, I discuss the work of critics from various disciplinary backgrounds and relate their insights to shorter vignettes drawing on different forms of media use, artistic practice, but also everyday visual culture. First, I problematise notions of difference that rely on a binary of invisibility and visibility, as seeing too little and seeing too much. I begin this section with a discussion of "colour blindness"—which is still sometimes presented as a naïve version of overcoming racial discrimination—by referencing the work of Osagie K. Obasogie with visually impaired and sighted individuals but also considering proposals for "colour-blind" casting. Subsequently, I address how this "blindness" towards difference can result in oversights in how digital media are conceptualised and continue to operate. I argue that the question of in/visibility needs to go beyond the surface of how we interact ever more intimately with digital media and also concerns technological development and a reflection of how these media function within global postcolonial networks of capital. Visual culture to a certain extent limits our imaginaries and is often complicit in forms of devaluing Others. To challenge such existing intersecting power imbalances necessitates a disruption of habitual ways of seeing at the level of looking at images and our identification with them but also at the level of producing different visual codes to begin with. Therefore, in section "Other Modes of Seeing, Other Modes of Being" of the chapter, I discuss post-representational artistic practice and "other modes of seeing" that contribute to a queering and transing of identification and the image repertoire as well as forms of refusing representation altogether. In this context I consider how visuality exceeds the realm of media representation and requires an interrogation of other "modes of being"[14] as well. For this purpose, I turn to the debates around a trans "bathroom panic" and questions of accessibility in the public sphere. In including such varied examples from visual culture, I hope to demonstrate the transdisciplinary potential of a revis(ualis)ing of intersectionality.

Seeing Too Little, Seeing Too Much

While revis(ualis)ing intersectionality, as mentioned, implies a certain scepticism towards visual evidentiality, it is not to be confused with an *un*seeing of difference, especially when this is invoked as a supposedly open-minded form of "colour blindness". To avoid what critics like Georgina Kleege (2012: 338) characterise as ableist references to blindness as "a prop for theories of consciousness", in which blindness is time and again evoked within philosophical thought experiments without engaging with the lived experience of blind people, it is important to seriously consider the actual modes of perception of those who have limited or no vision. Kleege is adamant that it is not helpful to insist on a binary opposition of blindness and sight, as congenital blindness is, in fact, quite rare among blind individuals. She argues, "It is clearly more useful to think in terms of a spectrum of variation in visual acuity, as well as a spectrum of variation in terms of visual awareness or skill" (2012: 345). This distinction is relevant because the term "blindness" is frequently evoked to denote a version of an imaginary naïve innocence. From the perspective of intersectionality studies, Osagie K. Obasogie's book *Blinded by Sight: Seeing Race Through the Eyes of the Blind* is especially instructive. In this study, he debunks notions of racism as based on "skin-deep" visual differences and calls for an "empirical Critical Race Theory" that engages with the ocular-centrism of the West. For this purpose, he combines insights from cultural constructivism with qualitative research methods. Having interviewed blind and sighted US-American individuals, Obasogie concludes from his sample, "blind people have a visual sensibility regarding race that is not unlike that of sighted people" (2014: 80). Many correspondents, for instance, recount events in school in which they became aware of why they were treated or supposed to treat others differently. The belief that white and African American blind people cannot grasp the concept of race/racism, disregards the fact that they partake in and are shaped by the culture surrounding them and that they possess various sensory skills to differentiate people. It belittles their abilities to understand the social repercussions of but also potentials for solidarity within racial positionings. This notion also trivialises how racism operates in framing it as a superficial visual problem and not as a mode of systemic oppression and exclusion with a long history.

That is why Obasogie is critical of a supposedly impartial "colour blindness" which is at times invoked by detractors of affirmative action. Giving preference to equally qualified candidates from underserved communities in college admissions or job searches is construed as an unfair advantage in this reasoning and colour blindness is imagined as embodying the ideal of meritocracy. This allegedly beneficial disregard of difference is also crucial in concerns for legal equality, as Obasogie elaborates:

> Colorblindness as a metaphor uses the seemingly concrete notions of vision and its absence—blindness—to give substance to the jurisprudence of non-recognition and a general ethos that law's refusal to 'see' race is the purest explication of its commitments to racial equality. (2014: 125)

The belief that race should not matter, especially before the law, calling to mind depictions of a blindfolded lady justice, can, despite good intentions, become an obstacle in efforts to redress structural inequalities, as Obasogie notes (2014: 128).[15] He argues that the references to an impartial progressive colour blindness remain "whimsical aspirations" based on "a desire to transcend the messy quagmire of race by envisioning a world where race is visually imperceptible" (Obasogie 2014: 125). The problem of racism would not be alleviated simply by the visual imperceptibility of somatic differences. To return to the insights of critical visuality studies, the visuality of race (and other forms of categorisations) cannot be reduced to empirical perceptibility, it is shaped by social interactions and historical regimes of knowledge production, which also account for different conceptions of how corporeal variety is interpreted as racial (and why blind people participate in these notions). While the historical legacy of chattel slavery, the "one-drop rule", and segregation under Jim Crow laws have shaped the strong focus on a Black and white binary in the racial formation of the United States (cf. Omi and Winant 2015), other cultures and localities have been impacted by different histories and nomenclatures to conceive of difference and here we could consider, for instance, how caste interacts with colourism in India which is shaped both by precolonial myths of "Aryan" superiority and a postcolonial legacy that is impacted by white beauty ideals and a globalised market of beauty products such as whitening creams (cf. Ayyar and Khandare 2013). This also demonstrates the need to reflect the famous intersectional triad of race, class, and gender from a more pronounced transnational as well as decolonial/postcolonial perspective (cf. Carastathis 2016; Collins and Bilge 2016).

Nonetheless, while a naïve version of colour blindness seems unsuited to achieve more intersectional justice, there are, of course, occasions where the visual remarkability of difference can be a hindrance to more fair treatment and should be disregarded in order to provide greater accessibility. Accordingly, colour blindness is not only evoked in conservative attempts to push back against anti-discrimination legislation. It has also gained prominence in debates around so-called colour-blind casting, sometimes also referred to more neutrally as "nontraditional casting" (cf. Pao 2010: 3–5). The reasoning here is to give a more diverse range of actors the chance to audition for roles that were not specifically written with a person of colour in mind.[16] Such colour-blind casting and gender reversals are increasingly more common in theatrical productions of canonical texts that traditionally include few or no parts for women and/or non-white actors. Moreover, there are now also guidelines to not specify external physical attributes of a character in a screenplay if this is not relevant for the plot to ensure different actors can audition for such roles. Obviously, such casting will not simply erase the socially informed viewing practices of audiences. While it is important to decouple acting from experience, the exclusion of non-white perspectives in the performing arts has limited which stories have been told in the past. This example once more underscores that it is important to become aware of, to *see*, difference to address social inequality rather than hold on to a supposedly neutral disregard of race—even if that means to purposefully overlook how a role was initially conceived—because heteronormative able-bodied middle-class conceptions of maleness and whiteness are still too often the unmentioned norm which continues to limit accessibility in the acting professions. Accordingly, the pressure to cast more diverse actors in a variety of roles needs to be accompanied by a simultaneous effort to tell stories that are more inclusive of experiences of racism, transphobia, and ableism and the few roles that exist along those lines should not continue to be embodied by the same range of white abled-bodied cis performers. Previously, actors were often rewarded with prestigious accolades precisely for their ability to perform queerness, transness, or disabledness on the screen, which draws more attention to the spectacle of transformation than to the story that is told. This kind of conflation can even produce unintentional harmful effects, for instance, when trans women are portrayed by cis men as this can reinforce the trope of trans women as supposedly predatory "cross-dressing men". However, as mentioned repeatedly, we should not reduce an intersectional approach to visuality to questions of representation solely. Visuality does not only pertain to the perception or depiction of bodies or even our sensory capacities. It is also shaped by the technologies and media that are used to produce, consume, and circulate images.

This nexus becomes apparent when we consider how media are intrinsically racialised, for instance. Already in 1997, Richard Dyer discusses how media apparatuses privilege whiteness and to this day, the filming of darker skin tones requires additional care from cinematographers given technological limitations. Dyer states, "photo and film apparatuses have seemed to work better with light-skinned people, but that is because they were made that way, not because they could be no other way" (1997: 90). This kind of inbuilt technological bias continues to impact various technologies. Obasogie mentions a Nikon digital camera that kept asking users if they "blinked" when they took portraits of Asian people and sensors of various devices that failed to detect Black bodies properly or not at all. Another example Obasogie provides is the by now discontinued Microsoft Kinect motion sensing input device which was part of the Xbox 360 console. This device which looks similar to a large webcam was added to the gaming console, it directly captured the movement of players via camera, microphone, and infrared sensors, and that let users control their avatars on the screen hands-free directly via their own body movements. Like other sensor devices, the Kinect seemed to initially perform poorly with non-white bodies (Obasogie 2014: 41–43). Such failures to program "computer vision" using AI (Artificial Intelligence) systems can be explained both by the predominance of white (male) developers and their (unconscious) assumptions that users would look like themselves as well as by the lack of diversity of test subjects and data (and this is very much a question of resources that are spent in development and training of the algorithms of the machines). Machine Learning (ML) is based on pattern matching and if one prepares the algorithm with initially biased information, this will only be aggravated over time. While the technology of the sensors would not respond properly to the real-life variety of its users, players, however, could easily personalise their avatars reflecting a wide palate of skin tones and body types on the same gaming console. This offer of diverse options is by now also common in emojis that are used on numerous digital communication platforms. Both are examples of what one could call (a kind of "United Colors of Benetton") surface diversity that simply multiplies the options. Whilst catering to varied consumers on the level of more representative digital interfaces, this surface diversity does not confront the simultaneous deeply flawed power imbalance in the materiality of how techno-capitalism operates in producing technologies and devices with which we interact more and more extensively and intimately in our daily lives. The rapidly progressing development of self-driving cars but also forms of automated surveillance of public spaces, for instance, like the gaming console, are based on a range of sensors and their interaction with AI algorithms. The lack of proper recognition of darker-skinned people that continues to sway the development of such technological tools is thus not simply an aesthetic issue of demanding better representation of non-white bodies but could potentially have lethal effects. Representation and recognition thus affect different dimensions of technological and media development that each requires an intersectional enquiry into how they operate.

Tressie McMillan Cottom, for example, highlights the tensions between privacy and hypervisibility that shape the Internet use of marginalised communities. While early cyberfeminism often imagined an optimistic version of a utopian "gender free" world wide web, we now learn more and more about "algorithmic stratification" (McMillan Cottom 2016: 211). In her intersectional analysis of online for-profit education in the US, McMillan Cottom argues that it is specifically lower income women of colour who are being coaxed into taking up more and more debt to invest in their education through targeted advertising on proprietary platforms. In this way, social inequalities are in fact exacerbated. McMillan Cottom explains, "algorithms [...] stratify group-based access to critical institutions such as markets, financial institutions, education, and work. [...] These differences were as much about categorical power relationships as about individual identity. [...] What we do online is, in part, about who we are categorically when we do it" (2016: 218). Thus, there remains an insoluble tension between seeking connection, to be recognised as someone with similar experiences and needs, as women of colour did in closed Facebook groups to exchange information about education and professional development, and the ways in which capitalist technology controls and stratifies the access to resources, by using the demographic data of the participants in such groups to place targeted ads. An intersectional interrogation of social media thus needs to combine the interest in the representational dimension with an awareness of the materiality and economic structures that enable and stratify digital visibility.

The notion of socially homogenous groups and their relation to identity categories and/or identification however do not always correspond to the ways in which digital media have also changed our perception of social interactions and intimacies. Shaka McGlotten, one of the speakers in the "conversations" series that preceded this publication (cf. Chap. 3), underlines the contemporary digitally mediated nature of (queer) virtual intimacies which should not be simply derided as "less real". Digital media promise evermore customised content and experiences and one cannot underestimate the affective allure that these digitally mediated forms of interaction exude. On the one hand, McGlotten argues, chat rooms, instant messaging, social media platforms, dating sites, and hook-up apps, enable users to evade "sexuality as a kind of identitarian demand". Users of such technologies do not need to be "out" or legible as "gay" and instead often seek fleeting experiences and relations to create new forms of virtual and non-virtual intimacies. On the other hand, the digitally mediated search for specific forms of sexual encounters and publics nonetheless reproduces hierarchical identitarian exclusions (most notably by pre-sorting possible matches according to age, ability, and race, e.g.). In McGlotten's words, "if people entered in the qualities they thought they wanted in a search engine, they would be less open to other possibilities that might occur in real world queer spaces" (2013: 6). Digital intimacies are hence both regulated by technological constrictions and human bias, but they also hold the potential for encounters across pre-defined identities and borders.

Stephanie Comilang's short science-fiction documentary *Lumapit Sa Akin, Paraiso* (*Come to Me, Paradise*) (2016), which was screened during one of the "conversations" events, focuses on different digitally mediated social connections which Filipina migrant workers establish in Central Hong Kong. As Tiara Roxanne describes in greater detail in Chap. 3, the film, which can be read as a sci-fi exploration of the community-building potential of digital communication, prompted us to reflect on the tension of demarcating where similarity ends, and difference begins. A person's positionality can shift in relation to the geographical and national contexts one inhabits. Accordingly, critics such as Floya Anthias (2013) speak of "translocational" positionalities to emphasise social space rather than fixed social identity.[17] In this way, Anthias relates intersectionality more strongly to contexts of migration and can, for instance, account for changes regarding experiences of privilege and marginalisation within life stories. This kind of mobility in identity formation also matches what Magdalena Nowicka describes concerning her work with Polish migrants and their understanding of whiteness (cf. Chap. 2). Dealing with inner-Asian migration from the Philippines to Hong Kong, space and location, rather than supposedly evident visual markers of difference and identity categories, are vital to grasp the precarious networks of identification in Comilang's film. Sometimes shot in close vicinity to the protagonists via their interaction with their mobile devices, sometimes from the bird's-eye view of the drone hovering above, Comilang employs a meditative film language that centres on the affective structures of care and community building among the Filipina migrant workers. The women seek to connect outside of the confines of their employers' homes, claiming public spaces as a place for physical self-expression such as dance and meditation and the joint preparation and consumption of food. In the film, the women use the disembodied digital storage of the drone to upload their self-produced content. The drone (or ghost) "Paradise" promises connectivity apart from their daily chores. It transcends their current locality and creates a communal archive of their experiences. In this way, the women's mobile phones become an extension of their constricted mobility in Hong Kong society and a means to create conviviality with those with whom they share the self-created islands of shelter in Central, Hong Kong's business district, as well as those whom they left behind in their home communities. As this example underlines, while social media might transcend certain national borders, from an intersectional point of view, we also need to address the actual geographical and social forms of mobility that these media afford and the kind of often invisible postcolonial entanglements of economic exploitation they exacerbate (cf. also Bergermann 2012).

The 2018 documentary film *The Cleaners* (dir. Hans Block and Moritz Riesewieck) depicts the mental toll that the outsourced labour of content moderation for social networks and sites such as Facebook, Google, and Twitter takes on those who are employed by subcontractors in the Philippines. Having to review ubiquitous offensive and upsetting visual materials (live streams, videos, and images), these moderators only have seconds to decide if content should be labelled objectionable because it is deemed pornographic or part of terrorist propaganda and is therefore in violation of the community standards of the platform in question, or, whether said material falls under artistic or journalistic licence and freedom of speech. These digital workers are incessantly exposed to hours of harmful visual content so that most users are not confronted with the less palatable aspects of social networks in their daily interactions with such media. Both the disagreeable content but also the mechanisms of content moderation remain invisible. Our contemporary interconnected forms of communication and circulation of images thus are not simply free-floating globalised networks of ever more visual content but embedded in the manifold disparities between capitalist aspiration in the Global North and the outsourced "dirty work" in the Global South. These mechanisms are also embroiled in the increasingly complex competing national interests of authoritarian regimes which are trying to reinforce censorship of disagreeable political content as well as the competing attempts to foreclose the spreading of false information and propaganda. To develop the approach of "revis(ualis)ing" intersectionality further, we cannot stop at the level of ornamental "surface" diversity. We must consider that digital media are agents in shaping our conceptions of in/visibility at the level of technology development, social and intimate interaction between users that include both potentials as well as restrictions in terms of community building, and that they are also reliant on the global division of labour in maintaining networks of distribution.

As outlined in the beginning, visuality is not only a question of in/visibility (in the media) or seeing versus not seeing something. It also concerns the question of how vision is tied to the exertion of power within embodied looking regimes. The shortcomings that I have described in relation to digital media also affect the human gaze and how we perceive others. To be clear, the problem is not one of remarking physical differences. On the subject of cross-ethnic representation, Rey Chow importantly reminds us that stereotypes are not simply a case of benign misrepresentation. She writes, "Contrary to the charge that they are misrepresentations, therefore, stereotypes have demonstrated themselves to be effective, realistic political weapons capable of generating belief, commitment, and action" (2010: 53). Vision is far from neutral and the question of recognition often a matter of survival. In the incessant instances of police brutality against Black people in the United States and elsewhere, time and again children's age is supposedly "misrecognised", as in the 2014 murder of twelve-year-old Tamir Rice who was shot by a white police officer while playing with a toy gun in a park.[18] In another more recent case in 2021, police in Rochester, New York, called to deal with what was described as "family trouble", handcuffed a 9-year-old Black girl who is not identified by name in the reports on the case. The footage of the body camera video shows that initially, the girl resists being forcefully put in the back of a police vehicle. When she is finally in the back of the car with her feet still hanging out of the door, one of the numerous officers involved reprimands her, "You're acting like a child", to which the girl responds aggravated, "I am a child, [what] the fuck".[19] Instead of being perplexed by this exchange, the participating police officers do not change their harsh handling of the upset child. Clearly still distraught, demanding to see her father repeatedly, a white female officer eventually uses pepper spray on the crying young girl. Such cases of abuse and excessive force on Black minors, especially Black girls, are so frequent that the Georgetown Law Center on Poverty and Inequality speaks of "adultification bias" in this context.[20] The officers have enough time to visually inspect the young girl, they are even reminded by the child herself of her lacking maturity, but they fail to conclude from this that she deserves the same care that one would imagine should be afforded to a nine-year-old in mental and physical distress. In her book *In the Wake*, Christina Sharpe characterises this kind of continued devaluation of Black life as part of a mundane deadly climate of anti-Blackness that is even more far-reaching than the characterisation of such forms of discrimination simply as ethnic or racial "bias" would imply. Sharpe draws connections across time to depict "the paradoxes of blackness within and after the legacies of slavery's denial of Black humanity" (2016: 14). To comprehend the contemporary effects that race has on different bodies and the way we are seen and we see others, we need to acknowledge the longue durée of modes of dehumanisation and the ways in which the history of enslavement and colonialism impacts the misrecognition and brutalisation of Black and people of colour to this very day. Mobile phones, bodycams, and the distribution of such incriminating evidence on social media have amplified the voices of Black Lives Matter activists despite the still shocking lack of accountability for these violations. In addition to the social responsibility to look at such footage, hashtags such as "#saytheirnames" are an urgent reminder to acknowledge the lives lost to racist violence as lives that mattered, as the cutting short of potential. The relentless visual spectacle of Black suffering nonetheless remains highly ambivalent, and understandably, there is also a hunger to see other images and not to be confronted with such traumatising footage over and over. Artistic practice is one response to this desire and often functions as a realm of resistance, a visual means to respond to intersectional injustice and the need to be recognised. In other words, while I keep emphasising the limits of a simplistic model of positive counter images, there is, of course, a yearning for new visual imaginaries to move beyond the spectacle of Othering bodies that has historically characterised hegemonic visual cultures for far too long.[21] So, while revis(ualis)ing intersectionality requires a focus on the nexus of power, subjugation, and vision, this form of analysis is also invested in exploring alternative ways of seeing.

Other Modes of Seeing, Other Modes of Being

In the following I wish to complicate the question of representation and identification via a discussion of the potential of post-representational artistic practices, of disidentification as a queering of identification with visual depictions, as well as of opacity as the refusal of representation. Like a more complex understanding of in/visibility in relation to community building, representation and identification cannot be reduced to a mimetic model of recognition and misrecognition. Conceptually, we should be especially careful not to conflate diversity and intersectionality. One does not arrive at a more "intersectional" visual culture simply by depicting a range of "diverse" bodies (and this would tie in with my earlier critique of a superficial multiplication of options as a form of "surface diversity"). This becomes especially problematic if the focus is on the representation of a singular body. If intersectionality is represented as the visualisation of an individual body, one ends up reducing intersectionality to an additive model of visible markers of difference.[22] There is always vulnerability in showing specific bodies and thus representation, identification, and recognition need to be framed as more complex relational networks between different bodies and not limited to the fixed (visual) characteristics of a person. So, instead of fetishising individual bodies, a revis(ualis)ing of intersectionality requires an engagement with different modes of seeing and conversely different modes of being.

At the turn of the century, a new generation of African American and artists of African heritage rose to prominence under the label "post-Black" art. Instead of resorting to imagery of Black and white bodies and the visual representation of glaring racist violence in their works, post-representational aesthetics avoid the spectacularising fixation on Black bodies and Black suffering. As Nana Adusei-Poku (2021) argues in her study of artists that belong to this group, including Marc Bradford, Leslie Hewitt, Mickalene Thomas, and Hank Willis Thomas,[23] such creative practice does not neglect histories of racism but uses abstract aesthetic means instead of mimetic depictions of Black figures to visualise the experience of being Black. Bradford's "Enter and Exit the New Negro" (2000), whose aesthetic at first glance evokes abstract or minimalist art, according to Adusei-Poku's (2012) interpretation of the title and the usage of endpapers in this artwork, demonstrates a desire to transcend identitarian limitations of constantly being reduced to an essentialised racialised positionality that is tied to physical difference. The choice of materials, which are a staple in Black hair salons and used for permanent-wave treatments, are employed in a manner that produces a simple monochromatic grid but can still be deciphered as referencing a specific racialised experience since hair is an especially potent signifier within racist looking regimes (cf. Mercer 1994). Adusei-Poku relates Bradford's artistic practice to a queer utopian potential of becoming that is less interested in fixing identity but exploring different modalities of bodies in relation to each other. Abstraction can thus be a means to reflect on racialisation without fixing the signifiers of race on the body. In addition to such post-Black artistic practice, queer and transgender studies have also explored how fine arts, cinema, and visual culture more broadly can challenge modes of corporal fixing.

In *In a Queer Time and Place*, Jack Halberstam (2005: 97–124) reads a range of abstract paintings and installations by artists such as Eva Hesse and Linda Besemer as transgender art—not because they show trans people, but because they embody a trans sensibility or aesthetic—a way of not fitting into the confines of a cis and heteronormative here and now. Halberstam argues that visual representations of transness have privileged transsexual embodiment which can be linked to postmodernity's fixation on ambiguity. But in this way, the trans body is often reduced to a spectacular prop. Instead, Halberstam is interested in a "technotopian, or spatially imaginative formulation of a body" (2005: 101). Hesse and Besemer use abstract means to visualise forms of embodiment that are processual rather than fixed.[24] Accordingly, Halberstam reads Besemer's colourful abstract "paint sculptures" made from brushstrokes of solidified acrylic paint that exceed the confines of the pictorial frame as a queering of more controlled and often implicitly male ideals of abstract artmaking. This art is non-narrative, it does not index a female or transgender body and yet it intervenes into male-dominated forms of artistic image production (cf. 2005: 121–122). Such a focus on form is also something that trans cinema scholars advocate.

Moving away from the logic of the shocking "reveal" that has dominated popular TV genres and narrative cinema by voyeuristically disclosing the trans body, which, thereby, is reduced to genitalia, Eliza Steinbock explores more experimental aesthetics of aligning trans embodiment and cinematic image production. Focusing on "shimmering" as "a concept for change in its emergent, flickering form" (2019: 8), Steinbock argues that

> transgender and cinematic aesthetics alike operate through the bodily practice and technological principle of disjunction. More radically, within

practices of filmmaking delinking and relinking across the cuts, gaps, fissures take place in the normal course of cinematography, rather than being exceptions. This makes it the art form most suited to a politically advantageous comparison with transgender forms of embodiment. (2019: 6)

Steinbock refers to practices like the phantasmagoria that go all the way back to George Meliès's early experiments with filmic montage and optical illusions, but which can also be found in contemporary trans artists Zackary Drucker and A.L. Steiner's work in which they complicate linear notions of before and after based on the cinematic capacity to achieve instant change by joining different images. The juxtaposition of the neat before and after reveal is rendered less linear and more opaque through double exposure and duplex photography in the artists' collaboration in a series of photographs (Steinbock 2019: 54). Drucker and Steiner thus use formal means to challenge narratives of gender transition but do not entirely relinquish the trans body as the subject of visual representation. These brief examples show that a whole range of formal choices exist that can be utilised to challenge the hegemonic gaze on "Other" bodies, and this is also to underscore that there is no simple binary of mimetic forms of representation as inherently lacking and post-representational art as automatically progressive. There are different ways through which the image repertoire can be expanded to avoid an objectifying aesthetics.[25]

But even within the realm of more hegemonic forms of representation, marginalised communities have found ways of resistance on the level of identification with such content. José Esteban Muñoz, whose work was crucial in establishing the field of queer of colour critique, criticises linear (often psychoanalytically inflected) models of identification that presume a heteronormative pattern of desire in his analyses of film, performance, and art.[26] While post-representational art and trans artistic practice challenge the fixing of identity as bodily difference at the level of the visual text, Muñoz additionally queers the process of identification with forms of (visual) representation. Going beyond Stuart Hall's famous model of encoding/decoding that distinguishes "dominant-hegemonic" codes, "negotiated" codes, and "oppositional" codes (Hall 1991 [1973]), Muñoz is concerned with "bad objects" of identification. Muñoz mentions that queer men of colour, for instance, often imagine themselves in the position of the glamorous white Hollywood diva in film. But this does not mean that they uncritically wish to emulate white femininity. He describes this as a more complex form of "disidentification" with white feminine beauty ideals. These are queer desires that do not follow a strict identitarian logic (and are therefore hard to grasp in either a psychoanalytical or an intersectional matrix). Muñoz writes,

> queer desires, perhaps desires that negate self, desire for a white beauty ideal, are reconstituted by an ideological component that tells us that such modalities of desire and desiring are too self-compromising. We thus disidentify with the white ideal. We desire it but desire it with a difference. The negotiations between desire, identification, and ideology are a part of the important work of disidentification. (1999: 15)

In this sense, disidentification is an anti-assimilationist strategy that minoritarian subjects resort to in encounters with existing forms of representation. It is both resistant and productive in enabling alternative forms of desire that might not have been the intended meaning of a work of art. Representation and identification are hence not limited to a linear heteronormative model, and marginalised subjects have always found ways of imagining themselves into fictional worlds, even worlds that disavowed them (cf. Eve Kosofsky Sedgwick's (1997) notion of a "reparative reading"). Other ways of seeing can thus include the production of alternative imageries but there is also the potential of gleaning pleasure from forms of representation that are not made with a certain audience in mind, as Muñoz emphasises. Yet another strategy relates to a more radical refusal to be represented within normative orders entirely.

This refusal of representation relates to the juxtaposition of transparency and opacity. French-Martinican philosopher and writer Édouard Glissant (1997: 111–120) uses the visual metaphor of opacity to question the transparent logic of linguistic correspondence. He demands the right to not be legible within specific hegemonic codes and dismisses the notion of a standard language. Glissant highlights the ambiguity of literary translation and proclaims a poetics of opacity that cannot be reduced to one correct meaning. This also concerns the question of identity and the relational qualities of identity formation as well as the limits of ever being fully "transparent", even to oneself. Opacity also points to the tensions between interpellation, identification, and affect (cf. Gunkel et al. 2015). Kara Keeling elaborates on the "right to opacity" as both a strategy of artistic practice but also engrained in political fights of populations that are constantly exposed to violent modes of surveillance and seek to imagine another world apart from constraints of group classification:

> To insist upon a group's 'right to opacity' in sociocultural terms, therefore, is to challenge the processes of commensuration built into the demand for that group to become perceptible according to existing conceptions of the world. It is a way of asserting the existence in this world of another conception of the world, incomprehensible from within the common senses that secure existing hegemonic relations […]. (Keeling 2019: 31)

Such a counter-hegemonic insistence on the right to opacity can also be found in critical migration studies that are inspired by Deleuzian philosophy. Dimitris Papadopoulos and Vassilis Tsianos, for instance, mention practices such as the burning of documents or the strategic rehearsed responses to the standardised interview questions that refugees are subjected to. They argue that migrants negotiate demands of identification in ways that exceed conceptions of representation. They write, "Instead of visibility, we say imperceptibility. Instead of being perceptible, discernible, identifiable, current migration puts on the agenda a new form of politics and a new formation of active political subjects whose aim is not a different way to become and to be a political subject but to refuse to become a subject at all" (Papadopoulos and Tsianos 2008: online). In this way, the authors contest more radically whether political subjectivity requires legible representation. While there is a danger in romanticising the refusal of legible subjectivity within surveillant migration regimes as a form of active refusal and not consider it also as the result of a more fundamental disenfranchisement, I think we must recognise agency when it comes to migrants' tactics of resisting scripts that reduce them to idealised objects of an often sentimental and objectifying gaze. In this understanding, the right to opacity is another way of disrupting notions of politics and representation.[27]

So far in this section, I have discussed various alternative ways of seeing that challenge clear-cut identities: post-representational art, disidentification, and opacity, which already points more strongly in the direction of other modes of being rather than modes of seeing. Our understanding of visual culture and intersectionality therefore cannot be limited to image production and circulation in the media, and we should also consider visuality in relation to the larger public sphere. This finally brings me to questions of security and accessibility of public space that are intertwined with regimes of visibility (cf. Brighenti 2010).

In their 1998 essay "Sex in Public", Lauren Berlant and Michael Warner famously argue that sentimental national culture and heteronormativity are linked via a familial imaginary of the nation state. They explain: "Heteronormativity is more than ideology, or prejudice, or phobia against gays and lesbians; it is produced in almost every aspect of the forms and arrangements of social life: nationality, the state, and the law; commerce; medicine; and education; as well as in the conventions and affects of narrativity, romance, and other protected spaces of culture" (Berlant and Warner 1998: 554–555). Following this logic, normativity can be quite literally described as a "comfort zone" that excludes those who do not fit the mould. In *The Cultural Politics of Emotions*, Sara Ahmed similarly evokes the image of the comfort zone to explain normativity. She writes,

> Normativity is comfortable for those who can inhabit it. The word 'comfort' suggests wellbeing and satisfaction, but it also suggests an ease and easiness. To follow the rules of heterosexuality is to be at ease in a world [...]. Heteronormativity functions as a form of public comfort by allowing bodies to extend into spaces that have already taken their shape. Those spaces are lived as comfortable as they allow bodies to fit in; the surfaces of social space are already impressed upon by the shape of such bodies (like a chair that acquires its shape by the repetition of some bodies inhabiting it [...]). (Ahmed 2004: 147–148)

Heteronormativity is understood here as predicated on normative embodiment that, in turn, is the precondition both for recognition and for comfortable access to social space. Consequently, disrupting binary identity categories and modes of identification is not limited to artistic practice but is also significant in how we engage with our daily surroundings. In Ahmed's words, public space is already "impressed" by the normative iterative practices of those who inhabit it, and this extends to how it is visually structured. Signs guide us, but also represent socially accepted norms. They, for example, direct us to the bathroom that is supposedly appropriate for our gender.

The debate around the accessibility of public restrooms is thus one more pertinent example to discuss the visuality of the public sphere. One can, of course, begin with the signage that at times exceeds the traditional triad of "male", "female", and "accessible" restrooms for people with disabilities (and the icons depicting wheelchair users have been criticised precisely because of their "ungendering" of people with disabilities). By now, there are creative and playful forms of visual representation that range from multiplying the options, merging male and female symbols, or resorting to non-human bodies, such as animals, mermaids, and aliens. Sometimes signs also depict the installed appliances (a toilet with a seat vs. a urinal, etc.) rather than the assumed users of these. And while such representational multiplicity can be a step in the right direction, the problem runs much deeper than simply offering more inclusive visual signage.

Trans activists have been especially critical of how there is now generally a celebration of more visible trans (media) representation—at least within US-American and some Western European media—and too little engagement with the lived realities of trans people. Specifically within public spaces, the hypervisibility of trans women of colour can often be fatal. In the introduction to the collection *Trap Door: Trans Cultural Production and the Politics of Visibility*, editors Reina Gossett [Tourmaline], Eric A. Stanley, and Johanna Burton, write succinctly, "the question arises of whether visibility is a goal to be worked toward or an outcome to be avoided at all costs" (2017: xx). Thus, the solution to more accessible public space in this case is not simply a separately marked "transgender facility", as this would expose already vulnerable constituents to more potential public surveillance and scrutiny. There remains a fundamental ambiguity in becoming more visible within mainstream representation. Coinciding with the greater visibility in the media, there are also numerous attempts of policing public spaces as, for instance, in the various cases at the state level in the United States to legally regulate trans access not only to public restrooms but also to health care. What is happening in relation to this form of "bathroom panic" is not a new development at all. As part of this backlash, transgender people are vilified as a threat to the safety and comfort of others by resorting to worn-out tropes. Trans women are, all too often, stigmatised as "sexual predators", and cis women their "prey", following this transphobic logic renounced as "men in disguise" entering women's spaces. Trans women urinating in a stall next to supposedly innocent young girls is turned into a doomsday-like scenario by the conservative right and says as much about their imagination of trans people as of young women's status as victims in need of paternalistic protection (cf. Sanders and Stryker 2016: 780). Trans activists have taken to social media and provided funny memes against this bigotry using the hashtag #wejustneedtopee (cf. Koch-Rein et al. 2020: 3). Architect Joel Sanders and transgender historian Susan Stryker demonstrate that there are many historical resonances in this kind of policing: women were kept from entering the paid workforce by denying them proper facilities, there is the long history of segregated bathrooms and water fountains that excluded African Americans and against which the civil rights movement protested, and there was also a public panic around gay men posing a threat of "contamination" during the Aids crisis. Sanders and Stryker write,

> the public restroom stages the transformation of an abstract concern into a tangible threat, by virtue of it being a physical space in which so-called normal citizens are brought into intimate physical proximity with precisely those presumably nonnormal people whose expulsion from or invisibilization within the body politic underpins and enables our society's norms of embodied personhood. (2016: 779–780)

Instead of limiting access according to identity (and to avoid the cultural fearmongering around these debates as "politically correct" identity politics and culture wars), we should instead ask how we can imagine more inclusive public spaces. Do we need to order spaces according to a binary understanding of gender (identity) or are there more productive ways to imagine them as accommodating different practices (or modes of being)?

If we move away from identity and focus more on accessibility in the discussion on public restrooms, we need to shift from narrowly, and often voyeuristically, fixating on trans bodies and instead take seriously how we could make these spaces safer and more accessible for more bodies with different needs and potential impairments, including people who need to assist young children or the elderly. Judith Butler proposes to destroy what has been built badly as a counter-hegemonic strategy. Butler states, "Dismantling forms of oppression, for instance, involves a certain way of destroying what has been built badly, built in ways that are consequential in the damage they cause. So to damage a damaging machine in the name of less damage, is that possible?" (Butler in Ahmed 2016: 3). If we believe this is possible, we need to visualise these spaces as accommodating more than the binary of male and female, and what is required then is a better design that is mindful of different types of embodiment instead of simply better representation of bodies in regard to the visual signage. That is why Sanders and Stryker have teamed up with legal scholar Terry Kogan and founded the Stalled! Project[28] to propose concrete design and best practice guidelines for all-gender restrooms. Their design recommendations suggest different "activity zones" within a relatively barrier-free open precinct. In this project, they not only address trans bathroom access but also focus on design to reimagine the public restroom so that it is less restricted by the identity of the people who use it and becomes more broadly inclusive as an accessible public environment.

We can also extend this conversation to questions of global justice and the lack of proper access to clean water and sanitation in the Global South that also urgently require feasible solutions. Critics point out that the lacking access to safe toilets impacts a range of problems that aggravate specific vulnerabilities of women, such as the fear of being subjected to sexualised violence and rape, but also give rise to numerous health problems, such as kidney disease, resulting from bathroom avoidance (cf. Panchang et al. 2021). Once more, we see that the interrelation of visuality, identities, and intersectional justice require extended vocabularies of analysis that go beyond pre-defined categorical frameworks.

My final example draws again on our "conversations" series: Doireann O' Malley's film *Prototypes*. This film probes various constellations of psychoanalytical discourses around (trans)gender identity. Moreover, the film in its visual depiction of bodies navigating different spaces can also be understood as linking transness to architecture, as Roxanne explains in greater detail (cf. Chap. 3). The many over the shoulder shots of walking protagonists invite the viewers to navigate different spaces with and from the perspective of the protagonists. The film undermines how transness has been traditionally visualised, namely as a form of confinement to the "wrong body". With its inclusion of a kind of time-space portal, the viewers also travel across time with the characters. In this way, the process of transitioning itself is reimagined as a kind of spatio-temporal "time travel" that teleports the protagonist to another dimension. While walking through different urban spaces and entering and exiting different buildings, one of the protagonists talks about how testosterone has "opened doors" for them. Transitioning is a way of navigating new spaces that are shaped by different architectures. Similarly, Halberstam identifies a shift in trans studies "from the idea of embodiment as being housed in one's flesh to embodiment as a more fluid architectural project" (2018: 24). *Prototypes* is about such an "architectural" depiction of embodiment that can be designed and redesigned. Transitioning is not narrated as a linear journey of one singular or extraordinary individual. The film highlights connections between trans people and depicts a range of gender variance. *Prototypes*' protagonists navigate spaces alone and together and, as a result, the film is not restricted to a homogenous understanding of what being trans means or looks like.

This form of challenging fixed identity via collectivity, which implies an ephemeral understanding of spatio-temporal communion, is what the formulation "modes of being" gestures towards. It is inspired by José Muñoz's writing on a critical queer utopianism (2019). In the posthumous publication *The Sense of Brown*, Muñoz introduces the term "the brown commons" to underline the conceptual difference between identity and "a sense of being-in-common as it is transmitted, across people, places, and spaces" (Muñoz 2020: 3). Accordingly, "modes of being" are attached to shared struggles but also an understanding of "collectivity with and through the incommensurable" (Muñoz 2020: 7). In a way, O'Malley's film, which like Comilang's *Lumapit Sa Akin, Paraiso* employs sci-fi elements, asks its viewers to exceed the current limitations of political discourse. This is to demonstrate that "other modes of seeing" embodiment are inextricably linked to the political intersectional project of pushing the boundaries of accessibility of both real and imaginary spaces to imagine "other modes of being".

Concluding Remarks

As I have argued in this chapter, the question to what end visibility is used yields multiple answers. Sometimes visibility is evoked as a demand for more inclusive representation and a different kind of media access. At other times, visibility can turn into harmful hypervisibility and surveillance. Consequently, an intersectional analysis of visual culture needs to probe the nuances of visuality and come up with different vocabularies of critical enquiry which are oftentimes limited by our desires to fit into existing categories and established types of representation as a form of social recognition. Thinking through visibility and intersectionality can result in an attentiveness to hegemonic imaginations of difference and the concomitant forms of discrimination. But in this process, we should also consider creative ways of resistance that include alternative aesthetics, queer forms of disidentification, and the refusal to be relegated to positions of Otherness. Our examination of visibility should not be limited to intersectionality as the representation of identities and more diversity in the media; rather, it should focus more on questions of relationality and accessibility. This also means that we must take into account the material effects that visual sorting has within the unequal postcolonial distribution of power which, in turn, influences the development of media under the conditions of technocapitalism and the global circulation of images. In this understanding, more expansive, accessible, and just modes of being are predicated ultimately on a willingness for more speculative forms of seeing and imagining the world otherwise.

Notes

1. According to Kaja Silverman, the "cultural image-repertoire" limits "what is at a given moment representationally possible" (1996: 204).
2. In this context, Donna Haraway's (1988) critique of the "God trick of seeing" and her emphasis on "partial vision" as well as E. Ann Kaplan's (1997) notion of the "imperial gaze" have been influential in relating ideas of objectivity and vision to colonialist modes of Western knowledge production.
3. Christian Metz (1975) introduces the term "scopic regime" to describe a specific cinematic form of voyeurism which is characterised by the absence of the real referent, the object seen (in contrast to more immediate art forms like the theatre).
4. Mieke Bal emphasises that the study of visual culture should not espouse a kind of "visual essentialism" in which the visual is separated from other senses. Both terms, visual and culture, need to remain mobile and visual culture must engage the "'visual' as 'impure'—synaesthetic, discursive and pragmatic; and 'culture' as shifting, differential, located between 'zones of culture' and performed in practices of power and resistance" (2003: 19).
5. Formative work on the representation of the 'Other' and feminist/anti-racist critiques of the image repertoire and looking relations, include a.o. Hall (1997), hooks (1992), Mercer (1994), and Pollock (2003). Cf. also *The Visual Culture Reader* edited by Mirzoeff (2012) for central texts that shaped the academic field as well as Sturken and Cartwright (2018) for an introduction to the study of visual culture. Engel (2018) proposes a form of discourse analysis of visual material that they call "engaged" or "power-sensitive desiring ekphrasis" as a queer method of reading visual imagery.
6. Nicholas Mirzoeff explains further that visual culture combines methods from "iconology" (shaped by the work of W.J.T. Mitchell), which in German-language contexts is also associated with the term "Bildwissenschaft", and its critical interrogation of art history and the contemporary circulation of images as well as the study of the gaze and ways of seeing that are more prevalent in film and media studies (cf. also Schade and Wenk 2011). Departing somewhat in focus from a specific medium or object he, in turn, uses the term visuality within a framework that is now labelled "critical visuality studies" (2012). Mirzoeff's conception of visuality thus slightly departs from other uses. He writes, "*Visuality* is an old

word for an old project. It is not a trendy theory word meaning the totality of all visual images and devices, but is in fact an early-nineteenth-century term meaning the visualization of history. This practice must be imaginary, rather than perceptual, because what is being visualized is too substantial for any one person to see and is created from information, images, and ideas" (Mirzoeff 2011: 2). Following this notion of visuality, images and their circulation are tethered to cultural norms or "ideas". Drawing on Foucault, Mirzoeff (2011: 3–4) describes visuality as "a discursive practice that has material effects" and explains a three-fold operation of visuality: first, it "classifies by naming, categorizing, and defining", second, the resulting separated groups become a means of social organisation, and finally, the classification itself is considered "right and hence aesthetic", thus making it appear predetermined. Consequently, in his book *The Right to Look*, Mirzoeff explores anticolonial resistance to what he calls a colonial complex of visuality that exceeds the study of specific images.

7. Famously Judith Butler formulates a theory in which the notions of livability and intelligibility are linked and conversely, "power also works through the foreclosure of effects, the production of an 'outside,' a domain of unlivability and unintelligibility that bounds the domain of intelligible effects" (1993: 22). In other words, social recognition is tied to normative notions of categorical recognition which is why non-heteronormative bodies are excluded from the realm of bodies that matter.
8. Artistic methods are increasingly mobilised in academic contexts as a form of artistic research (cf. Haarmann 2019), often in ways that link aesthetics and politics. Multidisciplinary art projects such as London-based Forensic Architecture or the German Zentrum für politische Schönheit (Center for Political Beauty) explicitly engage with contemporary politics, using aesthetic means to render visible marginalised accounts of violence and human rights violations.
9. Michel Foucault's (1977) analysis of panopticism in *Discipline and Punish* was crucial for the development of surveillance theories.
10. Schotel and Mügge (2021) discuss the process of making a Third Sex "categorically visible" in legislation in Germany and the Netherlands.
11. Hortense Spillers' work elucidates how enslavement dehumanised Black women in ways that fundamentally excluded them from the cultural formation of femininity, namely as "female flesh 'ungendered'" (1987: 68). For a trans perspective on racialisation, cf. Snorton (2017). Carbado (2013) discusses the interdependence of race and gender by focusing on how femininity is already implicated in norms of whiteness, as "racial respectability and gender normativity" (2013: 841), which require of Black women in the workplace to be "quite literally making themselves up as women" (2013: 822). Somewhat infelicitously, in this analysis of formal equality

frameworks in law and civil rights advocacy in the United States, Carbado proposes the term "colorblind intersectionality" to refer "to instances in which whiteness helps to produce and is part of a cognizable social category but is invisible or unarticulated as an intersectional subject position. For example, white heterosexual men constitute a cognizable social category whose whiteness is rarely seen or expressed in intersectional terms. Gender-blind intersectionality [in turn] describes a similar intersectional elision with respect to gender" (2013: 817). Carbado productively criticises the oversight of privilege here. But because this is understood as the unremarkability or absence of race (or "colour"), as opposed to the often-criticised notion of an impartial "colour blindness" that can inadvertently marginalise marked positionalities, as I explain in more detail in the course of the chapter, the visual metaphor of colour blindness to describe unremarkable privilege in intersectional frameworks appears misleading to me.

12. In her book *Speculum of the Other Woman*, feminist critic Luce Irigaray (1985) evokes the Latin word for mirror as well as the gynaecological instrument of the speculum to criticise what she terms phallocentrism in philosophy and psychoanalysis thereby also pointing out the gendered imbalance in regimes of knowledge production. C. Riley Snorton discusses how the emergence of US-American gynaecology and the development of "Sims's speculum" resulted from experiments on enslaved Black women and connects this to the larger "plantation visuality" that is characterised by the "unrelenting scopic availability that defined blackness within the visual economy of racial slavery" (2017: 33).

13. In discussions of art and philosophy that are associated with the label "speculative realism" or the "speculative turn" (cf. Bryant et al. 2011; van Tuinen 2017) we can witness what the editors of the issue "Aesthetics in the 21st Century" of the journal *Speculations* describe as the "return to the origins of aesthetics as the science of perception and sensuous cognition" (Askin et al. 2014: 22). Writing in this vein decentres the role of the political in relation to representation. The more straightforward notion of identity politics via mimetic visual depiction is dismissed in these approaches in favour of "affective dimensions" in aesthetic experiences. While I also highlight relationalities and affects to develop more nuanced methodologies of analysing visual culture, the radical complete decentring of the human in speculative realism and associated schools such as "object-oriented ontology" seems less compatible with an intersectional interest in addressing social inequalities. Thus, the description of revis(ualis)ing as a "speculative" practice in this chapter should not be equated strictly with "speculative realist" philosophy.

14. Drawing on a range of queer epistemologies, Gabriele Dietze, Beatrice Michaelis, and I have discussed in greater detail the potential of "modes of

being" as a way of queering the categorical framework of intersectionality (cf. Dietze et al. 2018).
15. For a comprehensive discussion of the legal shortcomings of colour blindness against the backdrop of the O.J. Simpson case, cf. Crenshaw (1997).
16. By now, the popular Netflix TV show *Bridgerton* (2020–) is probably the most well-known example of such non-traditional casting. However, equating the overly pronounced visibility of Black and people of colour in Regency England here simply with the realm of escapist entertainment or a form of "politically correct" retrospective representation risks invisibilising the obviously fewer but still existing stories of actual Black people living in eighteenth and nineteenth century England, some of them, like Ignatius Sancho or Dido Elizabeth Belle, for example, also moved within aristocratic circles.
17. Anna Carastathis (2013: 949–950) proposes to strategically undermine the constraints of perceived group differences to reframe intersectionality as a politics of coalitions. She discusses the visual representations of sisterhood during the 1984 Somos Hermanas delegation visit to Nicaragua. In this instance, US-American women of colour emphasised their intersectional similarities in experiencing racism and sexism rather than their national difference.
18. The policing of childhood has also become a pressing issue in border controls of unaccompanied refugee minors at the borders of Europe. Carly McLaughlin shows that in the increasing criminalisation of undocumented migrants, "childhood is not a fixed, stable category which guarantees protection, but is subject to ideologically and politically driven interpretation, scrutiny and suspicion and can, ultimately, be disproved" (2018: 1759). This, in fact, puts migrating children under closer scrutiny and greater risk rather than offering more protection. McLaughlin argues, "The age-assessment process highlights how abstract idealisations of childhood have concrete, material implications for child asylum-seekers, not least because the need to prove their identity *as* children in order to ensure their right to protection *as* children means that they are often subjected to more intrusive mechanisms of bio-power than adults" (2018: 1765).
19. A redacted compilation of the police video can be seen here: https://www.youtube.com/watch?v=BtJNUg8Ao7s (accessed 5 March 2021).
20. Cf. The Georgetown Law Center on Poverty and Inequality's Initiative on Gender Justice & Opportunity where resources and studies by the initiative on adultification bias are made available: https://genderjusticeandopportunity.georgetown.edu/adultification-bias/ (accessed 5 March 2021).
21. Frantz Fanon famously describes his encounters with the dehumanising white gaze. Continuously being reduced to the look from the outside becomes a psychologically damaging internalised form of devaluation

because the Black person is thrown back to seeing themselves as the Other through the eyes of white culture (Fanon 2008, French original published in 1952). Rosemarie Garland-Thomson discusses how "extraordinary" bodies, such as the "physically disabled" and "exotic ethnics" (1996: 5), were put on display in the commercialised spectacle of so-called freak shows during the late nineteenth and early twentieth century.

22. Carastathis (2016: 117–118) argues that intersectionality is often reduced to a "representationalist" politics in which the intersection of race and gender is represented by referencing women of colour when, in fact, the categorical intersection of race and gender is characterised by the specific *invisibility* of and institutional failures to address the claims of women of colour.
23. Kara Walker, who combines figurative and abstract techniques, as described at the beginning of the chapter, is sometimes also grouped under the label of post-Black art.
24. In her dissertation on the "Erotics of Abstract Painting's Materiality in the Works of Lynda Benglis and Katharina Grosse" Noemi Yoko Molitor argues that "queer abstraction has moved 'queer art' beyond common tendencies to either equate queer aesthetics with figurative representation (the depiction of LGBTIQ subjects or themes) or to base queer readings of artworks on the biography or identification of their authors (works produced by LGBTIQ artists). While these lenses are crucial given the problem of gender- and heteronormativity in art history, they risk reducing the question of queer erotics to taxonomies and morphologies of 'otherness' once again ('this is what a queer person or object looks like'). Scholars in the field of queer abstraction have noted the capacity of minimalist sculpture to represent bodies as malleable and multiple and, in turn, to re-visualize gender as equally multiple and transformable precisely because bodies are not rendered in definite, decipherable form" (Molitor 2020).
25. In an instructive interview, artist Renate Lorenz, art historian Johanna Schaffer, and curator Andrea Thal discuss the limitations and potentials of visibility regimes in (queer) artistic practice (cf. Lorenz et al. 2012).
26. Psychoanalytical film criticism relies on a linear heteronormative model of identification in which the visual text predetermines spectator positions and consequently, in this logic, men would identify with the active male gaze and women are reduced to the passive spectacle of "to-be-looked-at-ness" (Mulvey 1989). Queer critiques challenge these assumptions and explore forms of queer viewing (Evans and Gamman 1995). Moreover, Halberstam discusses the potential of a "transgender gaze" that affirms transgender characters rather than exposing them. This transgender gaze thus also disrupts binary conceptions of the cinematic gaze (Halberstam 2005: 76–96).

27. I have already mentioned the vulnerability of child asylum-seekers that is one case in point (cf. endnote 18). Furthermore, in her discussion of "the art of migration", Nanna Heidenreich challenges the idea that to "represent" forms of migration is already political. Heidenreich addresses the "problems of making visible victimisation" (2015: 103) and emphasises the role of image creation within migratory practices as independent of artistic practice but as potentially mobilised through "processes of aesthetic reflection" (2015: 113). Cf. also Dina Nayeri's (2019) *The Ungrateful Refugee* for a critique of normative assumptions about migrants' affective responses to their new host societies.
28. For more information on the project, cf. https://www.stalled.online/ (accessed 30 April 2021).

Works Cited

Adusei-Poku, Nana. 2012. Enter and Exit the New Negro—Von unsichtbaren Sichtbarkeiten. *Feministische Studien* 30 (2): 212–227. https://doi.org/10.1515/fs-2012-0206.

———. 2021. *Taking Stakes in the Unknown. Tracing Post-Black Art*. Bielefeld: transcript.

Ahmed, Sara. 2004. *The Cultural Politics of Emotion*. Edinburgh: Edinburgh University Press.

———. 2016. Interview with Judith Butler. *Sexualities* 0 (0): 1–11. https://doi.org/10.1177/1363460716629607.

Anthias, Floya. 2013. Social Categories, Embodied Practices, Intersectionality: Towards a Translocational Approach. In *Interdependencies of Social Categorisations*, eds. Daniela Célleri Endara, Tobias Schwarz, and Bea Wittger, 27–39. Orlando, Madrid and Frankfurt am Main: Iberoamericana and Vervuert.

Askin, Ridvan, Paul John Ennis, Andreas Hägler, and Philipp Schweighauser, eds. 2014. *Speculations. Aesthetics in the 21st Century*. Brooklyn: Punctum Books.

Ayyar, Varsha, and Lalit Khandare. 2013. Mapping Color and Caste Discrimination in Indian Society. In *The Melanin Millennium: Skin Color as 21st Century International Discourse*, ed. Ronald E. Hall, 71–95. Dordrecht: Springer Netherlands.

Bal, Mieke. 2003. Visual Essentialism and the Object of Visual Culture. *Journal of Visual Culture* 2 (1): 5–32. https://doi.org/10.1177/147041290300200101.

Bergermann, Ulrike. 2012. Postkoloniale Medienwissenschaft. Mobilität und Alterität von Ab/Bildung. In *Schlüsselwerke der Postcolonial Studies*, eds. Julia Reuter and Alexandra Karentzos, 267–281. Wiesbaden: Springer VS.

Berlant, Lauren, and Michael Warner. 1998. Sex in Public. *Critical Inquiry* 24 (2): 547–566.

Brighenti, Andrea Mubi. 2010. *Visibility in Social Theory and Social Research.* Basingstoke: Palgrave Macmillan.

Bryant, Levi, Nick Srnicek, and Graham Harman, eds. 2011. *The Speculative Turn. Continental Materialism and Realism.* Melbourne: re.press.

Butler, Judith. 1993. *Bodies That Matter. On the Discursive Limits of "Sex".* New York: Routledge.

Carastathis, Anna. 2013. Identity Categories as Potential Coalitions. *Signs* 38 (4): 941–965. https://doi.org/10.1086/669573.

———. 2016. *Intersectionality. Origins, Contestations, Horizons.* Lincoln: University of Nebraska Press.

Carbado, Devon W. 2013. Colorblind Intersectionality. *Signs* 38 (4): 811–845. https://doi.org/10.1086/669666.

Chow, Rey. 2010. Brushes with the-Other-as-Face: Stereotyping and Cross-Ethnic Representation. In *The Rey Chow Reader*, ed. Paul Bowman, 48–54. New York: Columbia University Press.

Collins, Patricia Hill, and Sirma Bilge. 2016. *Intersectionality.* Cambridge: Polity.

Crary, Jonathan. 1988. Modernizing Vision. In *Vision and Visuality*, ed. Hal Foster, 29–44. Seattle: Bay Press.

Crenshaw, Kimberlé Williams. 1997. Color-Blind Dreams and Racial Nightmares: Reconfiguring Racism in the Post-Civil Rights Era. In *Birth of a Nation'hood. Gaze, Script, and Spectacle in the O.J. Simpson Case*, eds. Toni Morrison and Claudia Brodsky Lacour, 97–168. New York: Pantheon.

Dietze, Gabriele, Elahe Haschemi Yekani, and Beatrice Michaelis. 2018. Modes of Being vs. Categories: Queering the Tools of Intersectionality. In *Beyond Gender: An Advanced Introduction to Futures of Feminist and Sexuality Studies*, eds. Greta Olson, Daniel Hartley, Mirjam Horn-Schott, and Leonie Schmidt, 117–136. London: Routledge.

Dikovitskaya, Margarita. 2005. *Visual Culture. The Study of the Visual after the Cultural Turn.* Cambridge: MIT Press.

Dyer, Richard. 1997. *White.* London: Routledge.

Engel, Antke. 2018. Queer Reading as Power Play: Methodological Considerations for Discourse Analysis of Visual Material. *Qualitative Inquiry* 25 (4): 338–349. https://doi.org/10.1177/1077800418789454.

Evans, Caroline, and Loraine Gamman. 1995. The Gaze Revisited, or Reviewing Queer Viewing. In *A Queer Romance. Lesbians, Gay Men and Popular Culture*, eds. Paul Burston and Colin Richardson, 13–56. New York: Routledge.

Fanon, Frantz. 2008. *Black Skin, White Masks.* Trans. Richard Philcox. New York: Grove Press.

Foster, Hal. 1988. Preface. In *Vision and Visuality*, ed. Hal Foster, ix–xiv. Seattle: Bay Press.

Foucault, Michel. 1977. *Discipline and Punish: The Birth of the Prison.* New York: Pantheon Books.

Garland-Thomson, Rosemarie. 1996. Introduction: From Wonder to Error—A Genealogy of Freak Discourse in Modernity. In *Freakery. Cultural Spectacles of the Extraordinary Body*, ed. Rosemarie Garland-Thomson, 1–17. New York: New York University Press.

Glissant, Édouard. 1997. *Poetics of Relation*. Ann Arbor: University of Michigan Press.

Gossett, Reina, Eric A. Stanley, and Johanna Burton. 2017. Known Unknowns: An Introduction to *Trap Door*. In *Trap Door: Trans Cultural Production and the Politics of Visibility*, eds. Reina Gossett, Eric A. Stanley, and Johanna Burton, xv–xxvi. Cambridge: MIT Press.

Gunkel, Henriette, Elahe Haschemi Yekani, Beatrice Michaelis, and Anja Michaelsen. 2015. Anrufung und Affekt. Ein Gesprächstext über (Anti-)Rassismus und queere Gefühle. In *I is for Impasse. Affektive Queerverbindungen in Theorie_Aktivismus_Kunst*, eds. Käthe von Bose, Ulrike Klöppel, Katrin Köppert, Karin Michalski, and Pat Treusch, 101–116. Berlin: b_books.

Haarmann, Anke. 2019. *Artistic Research. Eine epistemologische Ästhetik*. Bielefeld: transcript.

Halberstam, J[ack]. 2005. *In a Queer Time and Place. Transgender Bodies, Subcultural Lives*. New York: New York University Press.

———. 2018. *Trans*: A Quick and Quirky Account of Gender Variability*. Oakland: University of California Press.

Hall, Stuart. 1991 [1973]. Encoding, Decoding. In *The Cultural Studies Reader*, ed. Simon During, 90–103. London: Routledge.

———. 1997. The Spectacle of the 'Other'. In *Representation: Cultural Representations and Signifying Practices*, ed. Stuart Hall, 223–290. London: SAGE.

Haraway, Donna. 1988. Situated Knowledges: The Science Question in Feminism and the Privilege of Partial Perspective. *Feminist Studies* 14 (3): 575–599. https://doi.org/10.2307/3178066.

———. 1989. *Primate Visions. Gender, Race and Nature in the World of Modern Science*. New York: Routledge.

Hartman, Saidiya. 2008. Venus in Two Acts. *small axe* 26: 1–14.

Heidenreich, Nanna. 2015. Mapping / Assuming / Exhibiting /Activating the Perspective of Migration. In *The Culture of Migration. Politics, Aesthetics and Histories*, eds. Sten Pultz Moslund, Anne Ring Petersen, and Moritz Schramm, 99–116. London: I.B. Tauris.

hooks, bell. 1992. *Black Looks. Race and Representation*. Boston: South End Press.

Irigaray, Luce. 1985. *Speculum of the Other Woman*. Trans. Gillian Gill. Ithaca: Cornell University Press.

Kaplan, E. Ann. 1997. *Looking for the Other. Feminism, Film, and the Imperial Gaze*. New York: Routledge.

Keeling, Kara. 2019. *Queer Times, Black Futures*. New York: New York University Press.

Kleege, Georgina. 2012. Blindness and Visual Culture: An Eye Witness Account. In *The Visual Culture Reader*, ed. Nicholas Mirzoeff, 338–346. 3rd. rev. edition. London: Routledge.

Koch-Rein, Anson, Elahe Haschemi Yekani, and Jasper J. Verlinden. 2020. Representing Trans: Visibility and Its Discontents. *European Journal of English Studies* 24 (1): 1–12. https://doi.org/10.1080/13825577.2020.1730040.

Lorenz, Renate, Johanna Schaffer, and Andrea Thal. 2012. Im Gespräch: Sichtbarkeitsregime und künstlerische Praxis. *Feministische Studien* 30 (2): 285–295. https://doi.org/10.1515/fs-2012-0212.

McGlotten, Shaka. 2013. *Virtual Intimacies. Media, Affect, and Queer Sociality.* Albany: State University of New York Press.

McLaughlin, Carly. 2018. 'They don't look like children': Child Asylum-Seekers, the Dubs Amendment and the Politics of Childhood. *Journal of Ethnic and Migration Studies* 44 (11): 1757–1773. https://doi.org/10.1080/1369183X.2017.1417027.

McMillan Cottom, Tressie. 2016. Black Cyberfeminism: Ways Forward for Intersectionality and Digital Sociology. In *Digital Sociologies*, eds. Jessie Daniels, Karen Gregory, and Tressie McMillan Cottom, 211–231. Bristol: Bristol University Press.

Mercer, Kobena. 1994. *Welcome to the Jungle. New Positions in Black Cultural Studies.* New York: Routledge.

Metz, Christian. 1975. The Imaginary Signifier. *Screen* 16 (2): 14–76. https://doi.org/10.1093/screen/16.2.14.

Mirzoeff, Nicholas. 2011. *The Right to Look. A Counterhistory of Visuality.* Durham: Duke University Press.

———. 2012. For Critical Visuality Studies. In *The Visual Culture Reader*, ed. Nicholas Mirzoeff, xxix–xxxviii. 3rd. rev. edition. London: Routledge.

Mitchell, W.J. Thomas. 2005. *What Do Pictures Want? The Lives and Loves of Images.* Chicago: University of Chicago Press.

Molitor, Noemi Yoko. 2020. Chrononauts in Chromotopia: Toward an Erotics of Abstract Painting's Materiality in the Works of Lynda Benglis and Katharina Grosse. Emory University. Unpublished PhD Thesis.

Mulvey, Laura. 1989. *Visual and Other Pleasures.* 3rd. edition. Houndmills: Palgrave Macmillan.

Muñoz, José Esteban. 1999. *Disidentifications. Queers of Color and the Performance of Politics.* Minneapolis: University of Minnesota Press.

———. 2019. *Cruising Utopia. The Then and There of Queer Futurity.* 10th anniversary edition. With two additional essays by the author and a new foreword by Joshua Chambers-Letson, Tavia Nyong'o, and Ann Pellegrini. New York: New York University Press.

———. 2020. *The Sense of Brown. Ethnicity, Affect and Performance.* Eds. Tavia Nyong'o and Joshua Chambers-Letson. Durham: Duke University Press.

Nayeri, Dina. 2019. *The Ungrateful Refugee.* Edinburgh: Canongate.

Obasogie, Osagie K. 2014. *Blinded by Sight. Seeing Race through the Eyes of the Blind*. Stanford: Stanford University Press.

Omi, Michael, and Howard Winant. 2015. *Racial Formation in the United States*. 3rd. edition. New York: Routledge.

Panchang, Sarita Vijay, Pratima Joshi, and Smita Kale. 2021. Women 'Holding It' in Urban India: Toilet Avoidance as an Under-Recognized Health Outcome of Sanitation Insecurity. *Global Public Health*: 1–14. https://doi.org/10.1080/17441692.2021.1882527.

Pao, Angela C. 2010. *No Safe Spaces. Re-Casting Race, Ethnicity, and Nationality in American Theater*. Ann Arbor: University of Michigan Press.

Papadopoulos, Dimitris, and Vassilis Tsianos. 2008. The Autonomy of Migration: The Animals of Undocumented Mobility. *Transversal—eipcp multilingual webjournal*. https://translate.eipcp.net/strands/02/papadopoulostsianosstrands01en.html (accessed 2 May 2021).

Pollock, Griselda. 2003. *Vision and Difference. Femininity, Feminism and Histories of Art*. London: Routledge.

Raengo, Alessandra. 2016. Life in Those Shadows! Kara Walker's Post-Cinematic Silhouettes. In *Post-Cinema: Theorizing 21st-Century Film*, eds. Shane Denson and Julia Leyda. Falmer: REFRAME Books. Web. https://reframe.sussex.ac.uk/post-cinema/5-5-raengo/.

Sanders, Joel, and Susan Stryker. 2016. Stalled: Gender-Neutral Public Bathrooms. *South Atlantic Quarterly* 115 (4): 779–788. https://doi.org/10.1215/00382876-3656191.

Schade, Sigrid, and Silke Wenk. 2011. *Studien zur visuellen Kultur: Einführung in ein transdisziplinäres Forschungsfeld*. Bielefeld: transcript.

Schaffer, Johanna. 2008. *Ambivalenzen der Sichtbarkeit. Über die visuellen Strukturen der Anerkennung*. Bielefeld: transcript.

Schotel, A.L., and L.M. Mügge. 2021. Towards Categorical Visibility? The Political Making of a Third Sex in Germany and the Netherlands. *JCMS: Journal of Common Market Studies*. https://doi.org/10.1111/jcms.13170.

Sedgwick, Eve Kosofsky. 1997. Paranoid Reading and Reparative Reading; or, You're So Paranoid, You Probably Think This Introduction Is about You. In *Novel Gazing. Queer Readings in Fiction*, ed. Eve Kosofsky Sedgwick, 1–37. Durham: Duke University Press..

Sharpe, Christina E. 2010. *Monstrous Intimacies. Making Post-Slavery Subjects*. Durham: Duke University Press.

———. 2016. *In the Wake. On Blackness and Being*. Durham: Duke University Press.

Silva, Denise Ferreira da. 2011. Notes for a Critique of the 'Metaphysics of Race'. *Theory, Culture & Society* 28 (1): 138–148. https://doi.org/10.1177/0263276410387625.

Silverman, Kaja. 1996. *The Threshold of the Visible World*. New York: Routledge.

Snorton, C. Riley. 2017. *Black on Both Sides. A Racial History of Trans Identity*. Minneapolis: University of Minnesota Press.

Spillers, Hortense J. 1987. Mama's Baby, Papa's Maybe: An American Grammar Book. *Diacritics* 17 (2): 65–81. https://doi.org/10.2307/464747.

Steinbock, Eliza. 2019. *Shimmering Images: Trans Cinema, Embodiment, and the Aesthetics of Change*. Durham: Duke University Press.

Stryker, Susan, Paisley Currah, and Lisa Jean Moore. 2008. Introduction: Trans-, Trans, or Transgender? *Women's Studies Quarterly* 36 (3/4): 11–22.

Sturken, Marita, and Lisa Cartwright. 2018. *Practices of Looking. An Introduction to Visual Culture*. 3rd. edition. Oxford: Oxford University Press.

van Tuinen, Sjoerd, ed. 2017. *Speculative Art Histories. Analysis at the Limits*. Edinburgh: Edinburgh University Press.

Zerubavel, Eviatar. 2015. *Hidden in Plain Sight. The Social Structure of Irrelevance*. Oxford: Oxford University Press.

FILMS

Hans Block and Moritz Riesewieck, dir. *The Cleaners*. 2018.
Stephanie Comilang, dir. *Lumapit Sa Akin, Paraiso*. 2016.
Doireann O' Malley, dir. *Prototypes*. 2018.

Open Access This chapter is licensed under the terms of the Creative Commons Attribution 4.0 International License (http://creativecommons.org/licenses/by/4.0/), which permits use, sharing, adaptation, distribution and reproduction in any medium or format, as long as you give appropriate credit to the original author(s) and the source, provide a link to the Creative Commons licence and indicate if changes were made.

The images or other third party material in this chapter are included in the chapter's Creative Commons licence, unless indicated otherwise in a credit line to the material. If material is not included in the chapter's Creative Commons licence and your intended use is not permitted by statutory regulation or exceeds the permitted use, you will need to obtain permission directly from the copyright holder.

CHAPTER 5

Conclusion: Revising Intersectionality

Magdalena Nowicka and Elahe Haschemi Yekani

Abstract In the conclusion of *Revisualising Intersectionality*, Nowicka and Haschemi Yekani underscore the need for a transdisciplinary revision of the visual anchoring of difference in scientific knowledge production. In cognitive and psychological research, the habitual use of gender or race as categories that can be accessed by relying on visual inputs needs to be questioned. In the social sciences, a careful analysis of scopic regimes of difference can help overcome simplifications both of social constructivism and of biological determinism. In analyses of cultural representation, circular explanatory models of stereotypes producing "bad images" which would be alleviated through "positive images" should be avoided. To this end, the authors suggest learning from artistic research and practice to assume another point of view and disrupt preconceived orders.

Keywords Intersectionality • Visuality • Transdisciplinarity • Categories • Impurity

This book is the result of a transdisciplinary dialogue about the role visuality plays in ordering people along categories of difference and the potential of this enquiry for a revising of intersectionality. *Revisualising Intersectionality* considers the resulting discriminatory effects of this sorting, as well as possibilities for disrupting visual preconceptions. Our endeavour was informed by the assumption that we need to radically challenge the supposed visual evidentiality of categories of difference and similarity, a goal which we understand as aligned with the demand for greater social justice. To begin with, we explored disciplinary differences in how to approach questions of intersecting and intertwined forms of discrimination. There is a more pronounced interest in the formation of habitual modes of categorisation in the cognitive and social sciences in contrast to a stronger emphasis on aesthetic conventions and normativity in cultural studies. But despite these different approaches, we identified a common productive potential for disruption, or what we have described as the need to "revis(ualis)e" intersectionality. This is based on insights both from our disciplinary perspectives as well as on the dialogue with Tiara Roxanne and our interlocutors in the "conversations" events that informed the research for this book, specifically in relation to artistic research practices (cf. Chap. 3). It was clear to us from the beginning that a simple proclamation that "categories are sociocultural constructs" would not suffice to help us understand how difference is anchored in everyday perceptions and the concomitant belief of its visual evidentiality. Since scholars are not free from this fallacy, we need to work towards a reimagination of the analytic use of categories in academic knowledge production more broadly.

The interrogation of the mechanisms of visual evidentiality thus is crucial vis-à-vis the ongoing tendency in intersectionality studies to rely on and reproduce essentialising categories of visual similarity and difference to understand discrimination. To counter a naturalising and fixing of bodies along hierarchical, often binary, categories, involves an understanding of categories as part of the production of a particular social—and, we would add, a visual—order, of assigning people to social locations (Anthias and Yuval-Davis 1993; Anthias 2021). Specifically race and gender are often invoked in ways that imply that these are already self-evident, self-explanatory, and universal concepts despite our knowledge of their socially constructed and thus dynamic and locally as well as historically specific nature. This criticism is not new, but it is seldom taken up more explicitly in relation to visuality.

Traditionally, intersectionality research approaches the problem of the essentialisation of difference via an emphasis of intra-categorical heterogeneity. In fact, as outlined in some more detail in relation to the formation of the field of intersectionality studies in the introduction to this volume (cf. Chap. 1), from its initial wider circulation in the 1980s and 1990s, the concept of intersectionality has highlighted the very limitations of an understanding of categories as distinct or simply additive. Intersectionality was introduced precisely to analyse relations of power in society which marginalise those who experience multiple and intertwined forms of subjugation that are often not legible within legalistic frameworks that distinguish between racist and sexist discrimination, for example. This insight however requires a continual reflection of how to describe the intersectional effects of categories and categorising rather than reproducing an analytical framework which reinforces categories as universal, durable, and discrete and then analyses how they interlock only in a second step. Accordingly, Floya Anthias (2021) urges scholars to correct the tendency of intersectionality research to treat categories of difference such as race and gender as both explanandum and explanans, and thus explaining the workings of race with reference to racism alone, or gender in relation to heteropatriarchy. Anthias (2021: 64) stresses that there is no equivalence between a population category (socially defined groups such as women and men, white and Black) and the ways in which group-making processes and inequalities occur. The central dilemma of intersectionality research, as Anthias (2021: 74) puts it, thus is how to navigate categorical separation and the idea of their "mutual constitution". She identifies this "mutual constitution" as a heuristic to study contextual and situational operations of power (Anthias 2021: 75). By locating the mutual constitution of categories of difference and similarity in the realm of actual social relations, in contrast to a level of social ontology, and by focusing on their interlocking effects, Anthias evades the trouble with categories and investigates the intertwined processes, such as racism and heteronormativity, instead. These produce positionalities (but not categories) of subjects as women of colour or underage working-class fathers, for instance.

A different line of critique concerns not only the question of the mutual interdependence of categories and how to put this insight to use heuristically, but rather a more radical dismissal of categories that are deemed oppressive. Such a proposal is discussed controversially in anti-racist scholarship in relation to the question of whether it is analytically and politically expedient to continue operating with race at all. Alana Lentin (2008), for example, proposes to speak exclusively of racism instead of races since it is racist oppression that produces and utilises racial categorisation.[1] She argues that analysing the motility of racism in time and space allows us to understand how it roots culture in nature, fixing ethnic, cultural, or religious differences within an oppressive system (Lentin 2015).[2] For different reasons, Touré Reed (2020) also dismisses race as a category of analysis.

In his view, race alone cannot explain the social phenomenon of racism, nor is there a simple causality between a person of colour's experience of injustice and race or racism. Treating race as an explanans, a tendency which Reed calls "race reductionism", essentialises race as a category and in turn misses to address the complexity of social inequality.

As these examples demonstrate, the "trouble with categories" is often considered in relation to their mutual interdependence[3] or the more fundamental concern for how categories themselves are complicit in fostering oppression. These conceptual objections that have shaped intersectionality studies to date, however, do not do away with what we have discussed as the "problem of visibility" that impacts discrimination and the experience of being discriminated against. Consequently, a revis(ualis)ing of intersectionality emphatically does not assume that we can—or should—naïvely unsee difference. Challenging the essentialism of identity categories or rejecting categories entirely might be a tedious and ineffective exercise if it is uncoupled from the every-day embodied experience of categorising and being categorised. Instead of rejecting categories, or criticising their essentialism, we believe a more productive form of disruption focuses on the question *how* essentialising and fixing proceeds through reference to visible features and a reliance on supposed visual evidentiality. Scientific knowledge production, too, is not excluded from such scopic regimes. To provide an intersectional critique of how visuality is linked to knowledge formation thus requires a more fundamental disturbance of established ways of perceiving and representing difference and similarity.

As Magdalena Nowicka shows in Chap. 2, the impulse to categorise is part of cognitive and affective processes. To assign something or someone to a category means to decide which feature(s) is/are essential in justifying the belonging within a category, and to ignore others.[4] As some features might be difficult to observe, atypical objects can be miscategorised; uncertainty is thus inherent to categories. The interplay of self-identification and ascription, for example, as a woman or a man, makes categorising fuzzy (Kalish 1995). Through the reference to visibility, categories appear more natural, and thus durable, timeless, and relatively stable. At the same time, the ability to "categorise correctly" is also connected to an inability to perceive intersectionally, and it is linked to a process of learning to notice some but ignore other features, to report about our sensory experience, and the way selected differences and similarities are represented. As Crary (1999) demonstrates with respect to the work of French impressionists, most prominently Paul Cézanne, it is possible to learn an alternative gaze that captures many seemingly disconnected areas of the visual field simultaneously. Such a way of seeing enables a visual synthesis, "the rhythmic coexistence of radically heterogeneous and temporally dispersed elements" (Crary 1999: 297), which we could consider one form of perception that would also benefit a more intersectional mode of seeing.

Some cognitive science researchers suggest that we might be well advised to analytically distinguish between categories and concepts. We share a concept of race or gender which is shaped by culture. It is thus contextual and specific to a particular time and space. This involves visual evidence (perception), but it is not identical with categorising humans, for example, based on their skin according to the intensity of its pigmentation from light to dark. A concept of race influences our decisions of how to categorise skin tone into a category of "white" or "black". Some visual categorisations are independent of concepts (Deroy 2019), but the relationship between concepts and categorisation is dynamic and not yet fully understood.[5] It seems that instruction can impact this relationship to some extent. For example, telling people that their reactions are biased by their concept of race influences the way they categorise skin shades (Travers et al. 2020). It means that through instruction regarding concepts, people can partly adapt their reliance on visual evidence in categorising similarity and difference. More importantly, such a distinction between concepts and categories in research designs and analyses would also constitute an important step towards implementing more intersectional academic knowledge production.

In Chap. 4 Elahe Haschemi Yekani focuses on cultural representation and critiques notions of colour-blindness and an overtly representational understanding of intersectionality. She argues that we do not arrive at a more intersectional visual culture relying on the depiction of an individual body as representing difference or the portrayal of multiple different bodies as representing diversity. In contrast to (often neoliberal) notions of surface diversity, post-representational, queer and trans artistic expressions, in avoiding objectifying aesthetics, engage not with categories of difference and similarity as given but instead with visual regimes of rendering bodies intelligible. Such approaches open up a space for new arrangements and relationalities of sameness and intimacy that do not rely on identities and fixity but that also do not neglect experiences of discrimination. As Tiara Roxanne illustrates in Chap. 3, artistic practice has much to offer when it comes to how intersectional research frameworks could be expanded. Art is often rooted in a shared experience and explores modes of becoming through practice rather than preconceived modes of being. In a sense, it points towards the potential for developing identity not as difference from, but in relation to another person.[6] But postrepresentational as well as queer and trans artistic practices are more than just a possibility for resisting being represented by someone else in ways which do not correspond to our identity, and thus regaining control over self-representation. Via its use of imagery, such art engages in a queering and transing of binaries and preconceptions. Both verbs queering and transing therefore do not simply mean the representation of queer and trans people but concern a more fundamental interrogation of how embodiment is understood within a cis-heteronormative image repertoire and what alternative imaginaries could be developed in their stead.

From our analyses, we draw the conclusion that a continued revising of intersectionality would not only require more emphasis on the mutual constitution of categories but an acknowledgement of their inherent indeterminacy and impurity. This is of course not limited to fields of research that are explicitly concerned with questions of intersectionality. We consider this an urgent form of self-reflexivity that is required more broadly across disciplines, including cognitive science. When intersectionality is reduced to a form of shorthand for political activism in the public debate, the epistemological potential of the concept as a more fundamental challenge to the production of scientific knowledge is cut short. This does not mean that there is no need for emancipatory political projects that rally around politicised identity categories. But too often, the idea of "political identity" is reduced to notions of "essential embodied difference". Therefore, we need a more pronounced exploration of in-betweenness and instability and of how this in turn modifies notions of identity. This has been a line of critique that is associated less with intersectionality research and more pronouncedly with queer of colour, transnational feminist, Latinx and Chicanx schools of thought, probably most prominently exemplified by Gloria Anzaldúa's notion of mestiza consciousness (1987) and María Lugones' critique of purity (1994).[7] Lugones criticises the fragmentation of individuals within the larger "hierarchical ordering of split social groups" that renders some individuals as "thick", that is, invisible within certain group identities, as opposed to those who are "transparent" in these orders that endorse a logic of purity (1994: 474). Lugones considers such fragmentation as "conceptually at odds with seeing oppressions as interlocked" (1994: 473).[8] In her discussion of intersectionality, Anna Carastathis also draws on this tradition and proposes a coalition of decolonial and intersectional feminism (2016: 201). The potential for success of such coalitions, however, very much concerns the underlying assumptions of each enquiry and their compatibility. Carastathis posits that the "hermeneutic question here is whether intersectionality constitutes a representational theory of identity (as the dominant interpretation assumes), or whether it can be understood more fruitfully as a critique of representations that rely upon extant categorial axes of oppression" (2016: 223). According to Carastathis, to arrive at the second understanding of intersectionality, the less dominant but more "fruitful" one, and the potential foundation for stronger coalitions, requires a framework which would be less concerned with the representation of identities and more with a critique of the categorical preconceptions underlying representation.

Despite the acknowledgement that the intersectional experience of discrimination (which brings about the invisibility—or "thickness" in Lugones' terms—of subject positions such as women of colour) cannot be entirely separated from the realm of political and cultural representation, such a critique of the representational limits of intersectionality in our view however is not just a question of political and disciplinary coalitions. Rather than imagine intersectionality in relation to visually perceptible features of people or a complete dismissal of categories, we believe intersectional research needs to engage more concretely and practically with how visuality is implicated in processes of producing in/visibility that hinder but could potentially also be mobilised in enabling social justice and more equitable participation. Intersectionality research tells us what the outcome of categorisation is. Categories of difference and similarity can naturalise, collectivise, binarise, hierarchise and inferiorise, and they build "blocks for unequal resource allocation" (Anthias 2021: 75). But intersectionality research rarely tells us *how* categories acquire meaning and operate. In *Revisualising Intersectionality*, we argue that categories like race and gender retain part of their power through their association with visual evidentiality. In other words, the categorisation of people into racialised categories like Black and white is predicated on a cultural concept of race that guides the visual perception of difference. To challenge this notion, intersectionality research needs to incorporate new vocabularies of similarity and interdependency that explain categorisation rather than risk an over-emphasis on difference.

Such a revision of the visual anchoring of difference that informs scientific knowledge production requires methodological rethinking and can yield different epistemological outcomes. In cognitive and psychological research which investigates biased, additive, or selective perception of gendered or racial difference, the very premise that the perceptions of gender or race can be accessed solely by relying on visual inputs needs to be questioned. In the social sciences, a careful analysis of scopic regimes of difference would help to overcome simplifications both of social constructivism and of biological determinism, which would be advantageous both to qualitative and quantitative scholarship. A focus on the visuality of gendered and racialised difference surely generates new insights around the questions of misperceptions, and their social impacts. In analyses of cultural representation, we need to avoid circular explanatory models of stereotypes producing "bad images" which would be alleviated through forms of "positive images". An intersectional study of visual culture thus requires more expansive methods and conceptual tools for analysing (dis)identification and recognition.

To this end, we propose that we can learn from artistic research and practice to see things in a different light, to assume another point of view and disrupt preconceived orders. In other words, we quite literally need more creative forms of intersectional research across the disciplines. In the context of artistic research, creativity is not limited to aesthetic innovation but is understood as a form of epistemological reimagination. Anke Haarmann describes "imagination" as a crucial technique of artistic research. Imagination does not refer to arbitrary fantasy here but to a process of deconstructive and projective knowledge production, as a form of testing new meanings within the realm of the possible (Haarmann 2019: 290). With this publication, we do not aim to produce one coherent new theory of visual intersectionality studies. But based on transdisciplinary curiosity and dialogue, we discuss numerous often radically diverging shorter vignettes in this book. The result highlights how different kinds of visual experiences and visual artefacts can help reimagine preconceived notions of categorical difference, demonstrating the productivity of a more self-reflexive and hesitant interrogation of the processes, rather than the effects of visual categorisation. By focusing on the nexus of the radical ambiguity of visual experience and the material—often discriminatory—effects of categorisation that operates precisely by negating ambivalence through ordering, we believe there is a potential to disrupt the predominance of an understanding of categories that reifies difference.

Comprehending how visuality works—neither as biological determinism nor cultural construction alone—helps us to expand the framework of intersectionality research and stimulates different conceptions of how to approach inequity. This also means that we need to continue to engage in transdisciplinary dialogue and come up with new methods to understand the role visuality plays in our conceptions of difference and the potential to foster other political imaginaries. Such a continual revision of intersectionality means to strengthen it radically.

Notes

1. Paul Gilroy (2001) also proposes to renounce race as an analytical category that reproduces rather than dismantles modes of oppression.
2. This also impacts how we can enforce anti-discriminatory legislation as is evident in the proposals to remove the term race from legal documents, as currently debated in Germany and already implemented in France, which is meant to signal that there are no biological races. There are varying opinions on what the replacement of the term race with a formulation such as "racist discrimination" would mean for the future of anti-discrimination law. Cf., for example, the public round table featuring Tahir Della, Natasha A. Kelly, Doris Liebscher, and Emilia Roig, of which a transcript is available here: https://www.nd-aktuell.de/artikel/1150347.rasse-im-grundgesetz-benennen-oder-verbannen.html (accessed 30 June 2021). For a discussion of colour blindness and racism denial in France, cf. Roig (2017) and Perkins (2019).
3. Cf. Walgenbach et al. (2012) who provide a transdisciplinary discussion of how gender should be understood as an interdependent rather than intersectional category.
4. The judgements on atypical cases, such as "a lion with painted stripes" which does not make a tiger, support the thesis of some sort of "essence" of objects or living beings (Keil 1992). For a discussion of the difference between typicality and category, cf. Kalish (1995).
5. Lakoff (1987) gives examples of how the category "mother", when attached to the stereotype "housewife", coincides with the concepts of birth, legal binding, paid employment, and nurture (Lakoff 1987) through which it gains a particular meaning. Thus, there is nothing essentially "mother-like" which would lead to oppression if detached from the concepts of housewife within the legal and economic regime of the gender-specific division of labour (cf. Hernando 2017).
6. Cf. Boisvert (2010) on convivial interrelatedness as a mode of relating to each other across difference.
7. However, it is important not to misunderstand concepts such as mestizaje or hybridity simply as an overcoming of cultural rootedness (and as standing in

opposition to Indigeneity, for instance) but rather frame them as a challenge to the colonial order to begin with.
8. Lugones also suggests several techniques of how to resist fragmentation. These include code-switching, categorial blurring and confusion, gender transgressions, infusion with ambiguity, practicing trickstery and foolery, and many others (1994: 478).

Works Cited

Anthias, Floya. 2021. *Translocational Belongings: Intersectional Dilemmas and Social Inequalities*. Abingdon and New York: Routledge.
Anthias, Floya, and Nira Yuval-Davis. 1993. *Racialized Boundaries: Race, Nation, Gender, Colour and Class and the Anti-Racist Struggle*. New York: Routledge.
Anzaldúa, Gloria. 1987. *Borderlands/La Frontera. The New Mestiza*. San Francisco: Aunt Lute Books.
Boisvert, Raymond D. 2010. Convivialism: A Philosophical Manifesto. *The Pluralist* 5 (2): 57–68. https://doi.org/10.1353/plu.2010.0001.
Carastathis, Anna. 2016. *Intersectionality. Origins, Contestations, Horizons*. Lincoln: University of Nebraska Press.
Crary, Jonathan. 1999. *Suspensions of Perception: Attention, Spectacle, and Modern Culture*. Cambridge: MIT Press.
Deroy, Ophelia. 2019. Categorising Without Concepts. *Review of Philosophy and Psychology* 10 (3): 465–478. https://doi.org/10.1007/s13164-019-00431-2.
Gilroy, Paul. 2001. *Against Race. Imagining Political Culture Beyond the Color Line*. 4th edition. Cambridge: Belknap Press of Harvard University Press.
Haarmann, Anke. 2019. *Artistic Research. Eine epistemologische Ästhetik*. Bielefeld: transcript.
Hernando, Almudena. 2017. *The Fantasy of Individuality: On the Sociohistorical Construction of the Modern Subject*. Cham: Springer.
Kalish, Charles W. 1995. Essentialism and Graded Membership in Animal and Artifact Categories. *Memory & Cognition* 23 (3): 335–353. https://doi.org/10.3758/BF03197235.
Keil, Frank C. 1992. *Concepts, Kinds, and Cognitive Development*. Cambridge. MIT Press.
Lakoff, George. 1987. *Women, Fire, and Dangerous Things: What Categories Reveal about the Mind*. Chicago: University of Chicago Press.
Lentin, Alana. 2008. Europe and the Silence about Race. *European Journal of Social Theory* 11 (4): 487–503. https://doi.org/10.1177/1368431008097008.
———. 2015. What Does Race Do? *Ethnic and Racial Studies* 38 (8): 1401–1406. https://doi.org/10.1080/01419870.2015.1016064.
Lugones, Maria. 1994. Purity, Impurity, and Separation. *Signs* 19 (2): 458–479.

Perkins, Vinecia. 2019. The Illusion of French Inclusion: The Constitutional Stratification of French Ethnic Minorities. *Georgetown Journal of Law & Modern Critical Race Perspectives* 11 (2): 181–203.

Reed, Touré F. 2020. *Toward Freedom: The Case against Race Reductionism.* London and New York: Verso.

Roig, Emilia. 2017. Uttering 'Race' in Colorblind France and Post-Racial Germany. In *Rassismuskritik und Widerstandsformen*, eds. Karim Fereidooni and Meral El, 613–627. Wiesbaden: Springer.

Travers, Eoin, Merle T. Fairhurst, and Ophelia Deroy. 2020. Racial Bias in Face Perception Is Sensitive to Instructions but Not Introspection. *Consciousness and Cognition* 83: 102952. https://doi.org/10.1016/j.concog.2020.102952.

Walgenbach, Katharina, Gabriele Dietze, Lann Hornscheidt, and Kerstin Palm. 2012. *Gender als interdependente Kategorie. Neue Perspektiven auf Intersektionalität, Diversität und Heterogenität.* 2nd rev. edition. Opladen: Budrich.

Open Access This chapter is licensed under the terms of the Creative Commons Attribution 4.0 International License (http://creativecommons.org/licenses/by/4.0/), which permits use, sharing, adaptation, distribution and reproduction in any medium or format, as long as you give appropriate credit to the original author(s) and the source, provide a link to the Creative Commons licence and indicate if changes were made.

The images or other third party material in this chapter are included in the chapter's Creative Commons licence, unless indicated otherwise in a credit line to the material. If material is not included in the chapter's Creative Commons licence and your intended use is not permitted by statutory regulation or exceeds the permitted use, you will need to obtain permission directly from the copyright holder.

Index[1]

NUMBERS AND SYMBOLS
#saytheirnames, 93

A
Ability, 2, 3, 24, 25, 79, 85, 87, 90, 118
Ableism, 3, 12, 87
Activism, 2, 3, 120
Adultification bias, 93
Aesthetics, 24, 66, 79, 80, 89, 94–96, 103, 104n4, 105n6, 105n8, 106n13, 108n24, 109n27, 116, 119, 122
Affective, 24, 57, 82, 90, 91, 118
Affordance, 27, 28
Ahmed, Sara, 15, 99, 101
AI, *see* Artificial Intelligence
Algorithm, 69, 88, 89
Alienation, 69
Anthias, Floya, 21, 90, 116, 117, 121
Anti-trans violence, 3, 61, 83
Architecture, 59–61, 102
Art history, 80, 104n6, 108n24
Artificial Intelligence (AI), 6, 40n1, 41n11, 88, 89
Artistic practice, 5, 6, 38, 56, 66, 82, 84, 93–97, 99, 108n25, 109n27, 116, 119, 120, 122
Artistic research, 7, 32, 55, 56, 66, 73, 105n8, 116, 122
Asia, 18
Ásta, 27, 28
Attention, 15, 30, 32, 35–38, 78, 87

B
Bal, Mieke, 104n4
Batchelor, James, 69, 70, 72
Bathroom panic, 84, 100
Berlant, Lauren, 68, 98, 99
Bilge, Sirma, 1, 83, 86
Binary, 3, 4, 6, 17, 18, 21, 30, 33, 55, 58–60, 62, 79, 80, 82, 84–86, 96, 99, 101, 108n26, 116, 120
Black Lives Matter, 93

[1] Note: Page numbers followed by 'n' refer to notes.

© The Author(s) 2022
E. Haschemi Yekani et al., *Revisualising Intersectionality*,
https://doi.org/10.1007/978-3-030-93209-1

Blackness, 2, 3, 7n1, 7n2, 16–21, 23, 30, 33, 34, 38, 56, 62, 63, 68, 69, 78, 79, 83, 86, 88, 92–95, 105n11, 106n12, 107n16, 108n21, 117, 119, 121
Black, *see* Blackness
Blindness, 25, 84–87, 106n11, 107n15, 123n2
Body, 3–5, 12, 14, 15, 18, 19, 21, 22, 30, 33, 36, 37, 39, 41n9, 56–61, 67–69, 73, 78–81, 83, 87–89, 92–96, 99–102, 105n7, 108n21, 108n24, 116, 119
Bourdieu, Pierre, 12, 24
Bradford, Marc, 94, 95
Brighenti, Andrea Mubi, 20, 21, 81, 82, 98
Butler, Judith, 101, 105n7

C

Capital, 84
Carastathis, Anna, 2, 5, 86, 107n17, 108n22, 120, 121
Case studies, 56
Categories, 2, 12, 55, 82, 115
Categorising, 12, 26, 28, 30, 117–119
Choreography, 69
Chow, Rey, 92
Cinema, 6, 57–65, 79, 88, 90, 91, 96, 102, 103, 104n6, 108n26
  See also Film
Class, 2, 3, 14, 15, 18, 19, 22, 24, 25, 34, 57, 73, 78, 83, 86
The Cleaners (film), 91
Cognition, 4, 12, 25–27, 41n10, 57, 106n13
Cognitive science, 4, 12, 24–26, 37–39, 40n1, 65, 119, 120
Collaboration, 73, 96
Collectivity, 103
Collins, Patricia Hill, 3, 24, 25, 83, 86

Colour-blind casting, 87, 107n16
  See also Nontraditional casting
Colour blindness, 25, 84–87, 106n11, 107n15, 119, 123n2
Colourism, 39, 86
Combahee River Collective, 7n1
Comilang, Stephanie, 62–64, 90, 91, 103
Community, 57, 58, 60, 64, 86, 89, 91, 92, 94, 96
Complexity, 2, 20, 23, 24, 31, 57, 82, 118
Consciousness, 28, 29, 58, 85, 120
Crary, Jonathan, 13, 36, 37, 80, 118, 119
Crenshaw, Kimberlé Williams, 2, 56
Critical race theory, 1, 58
Critical theory, 39, 40
Cross-race effect, 29, 30
Culture, 4, 5, 17, 18, 20, 22, 28–32, 35, 37, 39, 40, 77–86, 93–95, 98, 99, 101, 103, 104n4, 104n6, 106n13, 108n21, 117, 119, 122
Cyberfeminism, 89

D

Decolonial theory, 4
Difference, 1–6, 7n2, 7n3, 12–40, 57, 59, 62, 77, 79–87, 89, 90, 92, 94, 96, 97, 103, 107n17, 115–123, 123n4, 123n6
Digitality, 68
Discrimination, 3–5, 7n3, 19–21, 24, 28, 31, 81–84, 93, 103, 116–119, 121
Disidentification, 94, 96–98, 103, 122
Distinction, 17, 25, 26, 33, 80, 81, 85, 119
Diversity, 21, 57, 82, 88, 92, 94, 103, 119
Documentary, 62, 90, 91

E

Epistemology, 58, 65, 81, 106n14
Essentialism, 5, 18, 20, 118
Ethnic, 14, 21, 38, 41n8, 93, 117
Ethnicity, 14, 34, 37
Europe, 17, 21, 23
Evidence, 12, 21, 23, 26, 30, 39, 93, 119
Evidentiality, 3, 39, 79, 82, 85, 116, 118, 121
Exposure, 19, 29, 35–38, 57, 96

F

Facebook, 89, 91
Femininity, 13, 23, 83, 96, 105n11
Feminism, 2, 57, 121
Film, 58, 59, 61, 73, 80, 95
See also Cinema
Foregrounding, 34–38, 78
Foucault, Michel, 105n6, 105n9

G

Gaze
  male, 80
  scientific, 39
Gender, 2–4, 12, 14, 19, 21, 22, 24, 25, 28–35, 39, 40, 41n10, 57, 60, 61, 73, 83, 86, 87, 96, 99, 101, 102, 105–106n11, 108n22, 108n24, 116, 117, 119, 121, 122, 123n3, 123n5, 124n8
Gender studies, 1
Germany, 12–15, 18, 23, 37, 38, 105n10, 123n2
Gilroy, Paul, 123n1
Glissant, Édouard, 97

H

Habitus, 3
Halberstam, Jack, 59, 60, 95, 102, 108n26
Hall, Stuart, 24, 80, 96, 104n5
Haraway, Donna, 83, 104n2
Heteronormativity, 73, 83, 98, 99, 108n24, 117
Hybridity, 60, 123n7
Hypervisibility, 62, 68, 73, 82, 89, 100, 103

I

Identification, 82, 84, 89, 91, 94, 96–99, 108n24, 108n26
Identity, 2–5, 12, 19, 20, 23–25, 29, 33, 34, 38, 41n9, 57–59, 62, 64, 68, 69, 73, 81–83, 89, 90, 95–99, 101–103, 106n13, 107n18, 118–121
Ignatiev, Noel, 21
Image repertoire, 79, 81, 83, 84, 96, 104n5, 120
Imagination, 2, 4, 13, 100, 103, 122
Impurity, 5, 120
Inattention, 35, 36, 41n10
Injustice, 12, 31, 62, 93, 118
Interdependence, 105n11, 117, 118
Intersectionality, 1–7, 12, 24, 27, 28, 32, 34, 55–73, 77–85, 90, 92–94, 98, 103, 106n11, 107n14, 107n17, 108n22, 115–123
Intimacy, 58, 67–73, 89, 90, 119
Invisibility, 6, 78, 82, 84, 108n22, 121

J

Jim Crow laws, 86

K

Keeling, Kara, 97, 98

L

Lakoff, George, 22, 123n5
Learning, 28, 32, 58, 118
Lugones, María, 5, 120, 121, 124n8
Lumapit Sa Akin, Paraiso (Come to Me, Paradise) (film), 62–64, 90, 103

M

Marginalisation, 57, 62, 81, 90
Masculinity, 13, 15
Materiality, 4, 38, 88, 89
McCall, Leslie, 2, 5
McGlotten, Shaka, 68, 69, 72, 89, 90
McMillan Cottom, Tressie, 62, 63
Media, 1, 6, 56, 66, 68, 80–82, 84, 88–93, 98, 100, 103, 104n6
Media representation, 4, 83, 84
Memory, 28, 32, 34, 37, 64
Mercer, Kobena, 95, 104n5
Migration, 6, 20, 65, 90, 98, 109n27
Mirzoeff, Nicholas, 104n5, 104–105n6
Mitchell, W.J.T., 81, 104n6
Mixed-race, 18, 19, 40–41n8
  See also Multiracial
Multiracial, 18, 19, 29, 40n8
  See also Mixed-race
Mulvey, Laura, 80, 108n26
Muñoz, José Esteban, 96, 97, 103

N

Nash, Jennifer, 1, 2, 7n1
Non-traditional casting, 84, 87, 107n16
  See also Colour-blind casting
Normativity, 61, 99, 105n11, 116

O

Obasogie, Osagie K., 22, 79, 84–86, 88
Objectivity, 79, 83, 104n2
Ocularcentric, *see* Ocular-centrism
Ocular-centrism, 3, 79, 85
O'Malley, Doireann, 58–61, 103
"One-drop rule," 86
Ontology, 106n13, 117
Opacity, 94, 97, 98
Order, 5, 35, 39, 56, 57, 80, 82, 83, 87, 97, 101, 107n18, 120, 122, 124n7
Otherness, 4, 7n2, 103, 108n24

P

People of colour, 14, 20, 93, 107n16
Perception, 4, 6, 12, 19, 20, 22, 25, 26, 28, 29, 32, 34, 36–39, 40n1, 58, 65–67, 73, 77, 79, 81, 83, 85, 87, 89, 106n13, 116, 119, 121, 122
Performance, 6, 13, 14, 57, 69, 73, 96
Performativity, 3
Philippines, 90, 91
Philosophy, 4, 12, 26, 37, 40n1, 98, 106n12, 106n13
Pictorial turn, 81
Poland, 13–15, 17, 18, 38
Porter, Zander, 69–72
Postcolonial studies, 4
  See also Postcolonial theory
Postcolonial theory, *see* Postcolonial studies
Post-representational art, 96, 98
Power, 2, 4, 5, 14, 18–22, 36, 37, 62, 78, 80–82, 84, 88, 89, 92, 93, 103, 104n4, 105n7, 117, 121
Prejudice, 14, 29, 30, 32, 34, 99
Privilege, 6, 20–22, 32, 62, 88, 90, 106n11

Prototypes (film), 58–61, 102
Psychology, 4, 12, 25, 26, 30, 33, 37, 39, 40, 40n1
Puar, Jasbir K., 2, 3, 62

Q
Queer, 4, 13, 14, 66, 90, 95–97, 103, 104n5, 106n14, 108n24, 108n25, 108n26, 119, 120
Queer theory, 58, 68

R
Race, 2, 3, 6, 12, 14–22, 24, 25, 28–30, 32–34, 39, 40, 40n8, 41n9, 56, 57, 73, 78, 79, 83, 85, 86, 90, 93, 95, 105–106n11, 108n22, 116–119, 121, 122, 123n1, 123n2
Racism, 3, 12, 17, 20, 24, 82, 83, 85–87, 94, 107n17, 117, 118, 123n2
Recognition, 3, 4, 20, 21, 27, 28, 41n10, 79–82, 89, 92, 94, 99, 103, 105n7, 122
Representation, 3, 4, 6, 22, 26, 38, 39, 58, 59, 65, 66, 73, 79–84, 87, 89, 94–101, 103, 104n5, 106n13, 107n16, 107n17, 108n24, 119–122
Rubin Vase, 78

S
Salience, 22, 35–38
Science, 4, 12, 20, 24–26, 37–40, 40n1, 57, 58, 65, 106n13, 116, 119, 120, 122
Science-fiction, 90, 103
   See also Sci-fi

Scopic regime, 80, 104n3, 118, 122
Segregation, 5, 24, 79, 86
Sensory, 22, 25, 27–29, 38, 39, 66, 67, 85, 88, 118
Sepahvand, Ashkan, 65–67, 73
Sexism, 3, 12, 24, 35, 83, 107n17
Sexuality, 12, 14, 24, 58, 90
Shadow portrait, 78
Sharpe, Christina, 78, 93
Sight, 13, 79–81, 85
Similarity, 3, 12, 27, 28, 30, 31, 34, 39, 62, 77, 90, 107n17, 116–119, 121
Skin colour, 16, 17, 21
   See also Skin pigmentation
Skin pigmentation, 18, 19, 23, 29, 33, 34
   See also Skin colour
Social constructivism, 122
Socialisation, 13, 35
Social justice, 2, 82, 116, 121
Social sciences, 12, 20, 57, 116, 122
Sociology, 4, 37, 39, 40, 63
Speculation, 83, 84, 104, 106n13
Speculative realism, 106n13
Speculative, *see* Speculation
Steinbock, Eliza, 59, 95, 96
Stereotypes, 17–19, 30–34, 92, 122, 123n5
Stereotyping, 19, 30–35, 37, 39, 41n10
Stryker, Susan, 83, 100, 101
Surveillance, 57, 65, 73, 82, 89, 97, 100, 103, 105n9

T
Technology, 36, 57, 63–65, 68, 69, 71, 73, 81, 88–90, 92
Transdisciplinarity, *see* Transdisciplinary
Transdisciplinary, 5–7, 78, 84, 115, 122, 123, 123n3

Transgender, 7n2, 13, 58–61, 73, 82–84, 87, 95, 96, 100–102, 105n11, 119, 120
　See also Trans, Trans*
Transgender studies, 95
Transsexual, *see* Transgender
Trans, Trans*, 58, 59, 95, 96, 100, 108n26
　See also Transgender

U

United Kingdom (UK), 15, 18, 41n8
United States (US), 1, 2, 21, 40n8, 78, 86, 89, 92, 100, 106n11
Utopia, 61

V

Visibility, 3, 6, 20, 21, 35, 57, 66, 77–104, 118, 121
Vision, 3, 36, 37, 58, 59, 61, 79–81, 85, 86, 92, 93, 104n2
Visual cultural studies, *see* Visual culture studies

Visual culture, 4, 5, 77–84, 93–95, 98, 103, 104n4, 104n5, 104n6, 106n13, 119, 122
Visual culture studies, 4, 5, 80, 84
Visuality, 2–7, 7n1, 22, 37, 56–58, 62, 79–84, 86, 87, 92, 98, 99, 102, 103, 104–105n6, 115, 116, 118, 121–123

W

Walker, Kara, 78, 79, 108n23
Whiteness, 7n2, 14–19, 21, 23, 30, 32–35, 38, 40n6, 78, 79, 83, 85–88, 90, 92–94, 96, 97, 105–106n11, 107–108n21, 117, 119, 121
White, *see* Whiteness

Y

Yamamoto-Masson, Nine, 65, 67, 73

Z

Zerubavel, Eviatar, 35, 38, 78

The manufacturer's authorised representative in the EU is Springer Nature Customer Service Centre GmbH, Europaplatz 3, 69115 Heidelberg, Germany. If you have any concerns regarding our products, please contact ProductSafety@springernature.com

Printed and bound by CPI Group (UK) Ltd, Croydon, CR0 4YY

25/03/2026

02078175-0013